GEORGE W. FORELL

The Proclamation of the Gospel in a Pluralistic World

Essays on Christianity and Culture

FORTRESS PRESS   *Philadelphia*

To the memory of
Kent S. Knutson,
a powerful spokesman
for the gospel in a
pluralistic world
and a wonderful friend

Library of Congress Catalog Card Number 73–79354

ISBN 0–8006–1035–0

3795C73   Printed in U.S.A.   1–1035

TABLE OF CONTENTS

ACKNOWLEDGMENTS

Grateful acknowledgment is made to the following for permission to reprint the indicated essays:

To *The Lutheran Quarterly* for "The Proclamation of the Gospel in a Pluralistic World" (Vol. 24, No. 4, November 1972);

To *Faculty Forum* for "Varieties of Religious Commitment" (No. 43, January 1968);

To *Religious Liberty* for "Christian Freedom and Religious Liberty" (Board of Social Ministry, now Division for Mission in North America, Lutheran Church in America, 1968);

To *The Lutheran* for "God Is Dead?" original title, "Maybe Man is Dead", (May 11, 1966);

To *The Fourth R: Religion and the Public School* for "The Illusion of Neutrality" (Wartburg College, Waverly, Iowa, 1964);

To *The Christian Scholar* for "The University's Ethical Crisis" (Vol. 48, No. 2, Summer 1965);

To *Religious Education* for "Some Implications of the Axioms of Classical Protestantism for the Philosophy of Education" (The Religious Education Association, New York, New York, November-December 1959);

To *Religion in Life* for "Law and Gospel as a Problem of Politics" (Summer 1962, Copyright © 1962 by Abingdon Press);

To *Reform of the Criminal Justice Systems in the United States and Canada* for "The Criminal Justice System: A Theological Perspective" (Board of Social Ministry, now Division for Mission in North America, Lutheran Church in America, 1972); and,

To *Dialog* for "Particularity, Pluralism, and World Community" (Vol. 10, Spring 1971).

INTRODUCTION

It is with a certain amount of trepidation that an author presents a series of his essays which were obviously written over a considerable period of time to readers who will read them much later and in a different setting. If I dare to do so it is because I believe that these chapters present *one* valid approach to the eternal problem of the relationship of Christianity and culture. They are not a "new theology" but rather the effort to address the issues raised by a rapidly changing world from the commitment to the classic Christian faith, or if you prefer, the "old theology."

Once in a while I have been called upon to present this position as over against other points of view current in our time. I have done this gladly and eagerly because I am convinced that it is precisely the "old theology," the faith in the one God who makes himself known to us as Father, Son, and Holy Spirit and whom one encounters "only by grace, only by faith, only through the Scriptures," which deserves a hearing among all the new theologies, east and west, black and white, female and male, revolutionary and psychologically adjusting, which clamor for attention now. My obvious eagerness to accept pluralism means that I believe that they all have every right to speak their piece, but it also means that those who believe that there is indeed a "faith which was once for all delivered to the saints" (Jude 3) have the right and the duty to proclaim this faith openly and unequivocally as part of their contribution to the pluralist conversation (for it has long ceased to be a dialogue). I regret that those who claim to speak for the classic Christian faith seem to do so often with anger in their voice and with little patience for the many people who cannot see it their way. This is hard to understand for the very faith they champion asserts that it is by grace alone that this stance is a human possibility. I hope I have avoided anger, irritation, or presumption. I hope also that I have taken seriously the problems as they confront us in our time, from criminal justice reform to rapid change, and from the varieties of religious commitment found in every church to the ecological crisis that threatens the survival of the race.

Perhaps the chapter dealing with the short-lived God-is-dead theology, which grew out of a debate with Professor William Hamilton at the University of Colorado, seems dated, but I would like to submit it because it seems to justify my claim that the "old theology" is less transitory than some of the more novel and fashionable ideologies. The other papers were presented in as varied settings as the *Aula* of the University of Erlangen (Chapter I) and before a group of representatives of World Judaism and the World Council of Churches in a kosher hotel in Lugano (Chapter XII). Some grew out of my work with the Board of Social Ministry of the Lutheran Church in America (Chapters III and XI); some were presented to student groups at the University of Iowa (Chapters VII and IX). Chapter II was my opening statement in a debate with Professor Walter Kaufmann on the campus of the University of Illinois, and Chapter V was presented to a national meeting of the Faculty Christian Fellowship at the University of Chicago shortly before this group decided to disband.

These are admittedly occasional writings. They are here collected because I hope they demonstrate the possibility of the proclamation of the gospel in a pluralistic world, which does not minimize the gospel or trivialize the nature of the pluralistic challenge.

Iowa City, February 1973
The Festival of the Transfiguration   GEORGE W. FORELL

I

THE PROCLAMATION
OF THE GOSPEL IN A
PLURALISTIC WORLD

It is the consensus of Christians that the church is God's pilgrim people hopefully and faithfully marching into God's future. On this march, these people proclaim to each other and to the world the Gospel of Jesus Christ. Both the "preaching of the Word" and the "administration of the sacraments" are seen as part of this proclamation. But while this Gospel is an eternal act of God toward man, revealed once and for all in one particular country and among one particular people, the communion brought into existence and kept alive by the Gospel has conscientiously tried to proclaim this Gospel in a manner comprehensible to the world. This task was always difficult; the Gospel of Christ, the event of the Cross and the resurrection, is bound to be "foolishness to the Greeks and a stumblingblock to the Jews" (I Cor. 1:23). But the same Apostle, Paul, who made this observation also insisted that one had to become a slave to all men in order to win the more. "To the Jews I became as a Jew, in order to win Jews. . . . To those outside the law I became as one outside the law . . . that I might win those outside the law" (I Cor. 9:20–21). He became a slave to a pluralistic world in order to proclaim the Gospel.

It is here, following St. Paul's missionary advice, that we realize that a rapidly changing world demands a rapidly changing adjustment on the part of the community of the Gospel to assure the faithful proclamation of this Gospel in our world.

It would be trivial to belabor the point of rapid and extreme change in the last hundred years. We are all only too painfully aware of it. An American writer, Alvin Toffler, has coined the term "future shock"[1] to describe the reaction of human beings to this rapid and extreme change which they are constantly experiencing. We all know that a hundred years ago, in spite of all optimism about the future and confidence in technology, people assumed that their grandchildren would live in a world recognizably similar to their own. We are almost equally sure that the world of our grandchildren—if it exists at all—will be vastly different from ours. Toffler illustrates the death of permanence with examples from the impermanence of dolls to the impermanence of paper wedding gowns, cars, homes and finally the impermanence of all human relationships, as the crisis of marriage and the family so drastically indicates.

Some of Toffler's examples may not yet apply in Europe to the degree to which they apply in America, but if past experience is a clue, the situation in America is only the most advanced form of the kind of world a highly developed technology produces. (Parenthetically, political ideologies seem irrelevant to this technology–produced impermanence, e.g., marriage in Communist countries is, if anything, less stable than marriage in Western European nations.)

But while many aspects of rapid change have affected the proclamation of the Gospel, one situation in particular deserves our special interest because of its intrinsic importance for the proclamation of the Gospel, namely, the development of pluralism. Pluralism, the existence of various and contradictory approaches to life simultaneously, which can neither be uprooted nor overcome, absorbed or ignored, is the ideologically most threatening aspect of the modern world. It is so threatening because it undermines the notion

[1] Alvin Toffler, *Future Shock* (New York: Random House, 1970).

of "one truth" and thus jeopardizes equally the claims of atheists and theists, nationalists and internationalists, totalitarians and democrats. While we are here particularly interested in its theological significance, we should note briefly that it has wrought havoc with the homogeneity of world Communism, that it has threatened the underlying assumptions of melting-pot America, and that it has undermined the discussion of ethics, aesthetics, and epistemology.

Pluralism means, in the words of the American sociologist, Peter Berger, that "The man in the street is confronted with a wide variety of religious and other reality-defining agencies that compete for his allegiance. In other words, the phenomenon called 'pluralism' is a social–structural correlate of the secularization of consciousness."[2]

Pluralism has two dimensions: as a worldwide phenomenon, and as a reality within each culture.

As a worldwide phenomenon pluralism means that there are, in fact, many different ways of ideologically constructing and maintaining the world used by various peoples and cultures. As such, of course, it is nothing new. In a certain sense, the world known to us through the study of human history has always been pluralistic. What has changed in our time is merely that communications technology has brought these other ways of seeing the world very close to us. In the resulting world, people who see things in a radically different way have become our neighbors who cannot be ignored.

When this awareness of pluralism dawned on the people of the world they responded in two quite different ways. We could describe them as the way of the East and the way of the West. The people of the East tried to maintain their ideological security by cutting themselves off from the realm of false ideologies by a process of radical isolation. Most

[2] Peter L. Berger, *The Sacred Canopy* (New York: Doubleday, 1967), p. 127.

typically, the Japanese made it a capital offense to leave the islands of Japan and return again without special Imperial permission. Thus they hoped to overcome the threat of pluralism by avoiding all contact with the *Gaijin*, foreigners. As we all know, this defense failed. In the nineteenth century the Americans forced their way into Japan, bringing on what is called the Meiji Restoration, a forced process of modernization in order to avoid the colonial fate that had befallen India and China.

This illustrates the Western way of dealing with the threat of pluralism. The West tried to force its own ideology upon all the nations and make them conform to the Western vision and thus reduce the threat of pluralism for the West. This was certainly one important aspect of colonialism and imperialism. From the point of view of the Church of Christ the tragedy was that the Christian faith, which was deeply involved with Western ideology, became entangled in the Western effort to overcome pluralism by the establishment of a worldwide Western ideology which could avert this threat. The missionary movement has thus often been caricatured as merely the ideological aspect of colonialism. But while this was on the whole an unjust misrepresentation, there was enough confusion in the minds of the Christian community and of the missionaries themselves that they could easily be misused for such ideological purposes. One of the great benefits of the collapse of Western colonialism in our time is the extrication of the all-important worldwide proclamation of the Gospel from the ambiguous claims of Western civilization. Unfortunately, the terms "mission" and "missionary" may have been permanently corrupted by the close association between the proclamation of the Gospel and the "spread of Western civilization." It must be of special interest to us that the Christian communion's relationship to the Jewish people was paradigmatic for this eventual development. Here, too, Western civilization and Christian communion were so utterly confused that it was possible to describe Christian baptism in the early nineteenth century as the "admission ticket to Western civilization." To this day, the term "Christian" means in many places in Africa a person with Western education rather than a disciple of Jesus Christ. Indeed the strategic and tactical errors of the eventual Christian approach to the non–Christian religions were all rehearsed in the Christian approach to the Jews.

But this is only one aspect of pluralism. In the last few centuries, and especially in the last fifty years, pluralism has become a reality within each culture and to a degree within each individual.

In the past it was possible without great effort to avoid contact with other religions or reality-defining agencies. One could ignore the "lesser breeds, without the law," as Rudyard Kipling foolishly described the people whose different ways of constructing and maintaining the world represented a threat to the West. In the past, this had been successfully done to all aliens; they were called barbarians, infidels, heathen, and belonged to an anomic realm whose way of seeing things could be safely ignored. An inkling of the problem came to the surface for German–speaking people who use the same term for gentiles and heathen, *gojim* and *pagani*. Luther was aware of the fact that in relationship to the Jews he was indeed himself a heathen. But this peculiar awareness was of no general significance, and most people managed to ignore, suppress, or superficially dismiss the challenge coming from the other reality-defining agencies. This attitude has become impossible in our time. Indeed, the effort is still being made, as revealed by the remark to an American observer by an Egyptian engineer behind the back of a Russian colleague in modern Cairo, that he as a Muslim could not possibly take Marxism seriously, which he described as "the atheist ideology concocted by a renegade German Jew." But this very language only tried to hide the felt threat from the other reality-defining agency which had become so real in the land of the Pharaohs. Similarly, we note that American students from Christian families learn how to pray from a Hindu guru, while American students from Jewish families join the "Jesus Freaks." In America we have black Jewish leaders and Zen Buddhists of Swedish Lutheran background. Again, it may be true that the pluralistic confrontation is most advanced in the United States, but it is only a question of time until the mass media and total communications produce the same confrontation everywhere in the world. Any effort to avoid this development by isolation through the use of physical or spiritual walls will prove as ineffective in the long run as the famous Chinese wall.

But pluralism is not only among us, it is also within us. Each of us, bombarded by these many reality-defining possibilities, is tempted to create his own syncretistic worldview, picking and choosing the combination which meets his needs. Pluralism becomes internalized, and the confrontation of the various reality-defining agencies takes place within us. The results may be personal monstrosities like "Christian atheism" or nature worship advertised as Christian hope, to give only two examples. Nostalgia for the good old days in which fewer options or no real options at all made decisions easier is not helpful. Pluralism is here to stay. The Christian Gospel has to be proclaimed within its context. Again, only the confrontation with Judaism gives us any clue to the manner in which the Christian community reacted to such a confrontation in the past. But this look backward is by no means encouraging. Can we learn from the errors of the past?

While the answer to this question will be gained in the life of the Christian communion in the next hundred years, there is a clarification of the task of proclaiming the Gospel in a pluralistic world, which may prove of some help in the future. The discussion of the relationship between Christianity and other reality-defining agencies in the past generation has been clouded by the inconclusive quarrel over Christianity and religion, which produced first the claim that Christianity is the highest religion in some evolutionary sense and later the assertion that Christianity is not a religion at all and the discovery of "religionless Christianity." It seems apparent if one looks at the phenomenon Christianity that it is a religion, if the term religion has any meaning at all, and that its evaluation in comparison with other religions depends on the standards one uses. This made the debates between Jews, Christians, and Muslims always inconclusive. But Christianity has survived as a religion because the people who called themselves Christians were able to find religious expressions for their Christian claims. It is as a religion, however, that Christianity is particularly involved in and threatened by the world of pluralism. As a religion, Christianity has many dimensions each with its own reality-defining claims, of which some have received a disproportionate share of attention; and this has tended to obscure our understanding of Christianity.

All religions have at least four major dimensions: a cognitive dimension which supplies propositions to which one assents; a moral dimension which suggests a way of life which one follows; an emotional dimension which produces feelings which one expresses in a variety of ways; and a communal dimension which involves us in relationships which identify, support, and obligate us. Christianity, in general, and all its confessional subdivisions are involved in all these dimensions of Christianity as religion, and it would be possible to distinguish between various confessions according to the emphasis placed on each of these dimensions and the particular mix they represent. In addition, there is a tendency on the part of theologians to exaggerate the significance of the first aspect: religion as a cognitive system. Since theologians generally have written the history of Christianity, there has been a tendency to see its development from the point of view of the cognitive dimension, a particular concern of theologians, almost to the exclusion of the other three dimensions. For example, faith, an important aspect of all religion, has in the history of Christian theology received a peculiarly cognitive emphasis which practically identifies it with assent to propositions. While the theologians themselves were often aware of the inadequacy of this definition and tried to guard against it, such subtleties were generally lost in the translation into ordinary speech. The result is that the man in the street, both Christian and non–Christian, sees faith still as assent to propositions.

Yet it is quite obvious that people all over the world claim to be Christians for reasons that have little to do with any particular Christian propositions. For many, Christianity produces a moral universe that they affirm—even if they do not live up to their affirmation. In the United States, for example, large numbers of people who actively support the church with substantial gifts are ignorant and unconcerned about Christianity as a belief–system, but regard it highly as a way of life. It was this observation of the significance of Christian ideals for people quite unfamiliar with Christian theology which led Reinhold Niebuhr to speak of the "relevance of an impossible ethical ideal." Ignorant of even the most rudimentary propositions of the Christian faith, such people are active in the life of the Christian community and consider themselves devoted and sincere Christians, followers of Christ, eager to carry on the Christian style of life. If pressed by the more theologically oriented, they will render lip service to the cognitive propositions which they either do not understand or consider irrelevant or at best symbolic devices to exclude outsiders, thus functioning in the manner of the famous *shiboleth* in the Old Testament (Judg. 12:6). It would appear that this understanding of Christianity under the dominance of the moral dimension is as important for the history of the Christian church as the more frequently studied cognitive dimension. Not only in America but all over the world many people see Christianity primarily as a way of life which one follows. Especially in the missionary outreach of the church it has been this moral dimension that has been decisive. Those who have converted to Christianity did so because they considered it morally superior to other religious options available to them. Even in the encounter between Jews and Christians it was often the moral dimension that was emphasized, and some of the earliest participants in the confrontation between church and synagogue claimed moral superiority for their particular cause. Reform movements within Christianity, including the predecessors of the Reformation, Wycliffe and Hus, were particularly concerned about the moral decline of the church. And in the nineteenth and twentieth centuries many people continued to admire the moral dimension of the life of Jesus long after they had discarded his theological claims.

But what about the third dimension, the emotional dimension? For the American student of Christianity the emotional dimension seems strikingly significant. The great revivals of Christianity in America were always undergirded by the emotional needs and experiences of vast masses of people. The expressions of these feelings were often bizarre. Quaking, shaking, ranting, shouting, and speaking in tongues were part of their Christian worship and still are in many places. But even in Europe, Pietism and the worship of Zinzendorf's *Brüdergemeine* met profound emotional needs, and it is certainly no accident that the dominant theological figure of the nineteenth century, Schleiermacher, was educated at Niesky and Barby under the auspices of the *Brüdergemeine* and called himself *einen Herrnhuter von einer höheren Ordnung,* "a Moravian of a higher order."

Nobody who has felt the incredible pathos of the music of Bach will deny the emotional dimension of the Christian faith. It was his awareness of the complexity and richness

of the Christian faith which made Nathan Soderblom refer
to Bach as the Fifth Evangelist.

Here again a more inclusive study of the history of Christianity, one not almost exclusively concerned with the cognitive dimension of the Christian faith, would note the power
of the emotions and feelings in gathering men and women
into the Christian communion. Some of the mass conver-
sions from Pentecost to contemporary Africa, Asia, and
America can be understood only if this emotional dimension of Christianity is given its due emphasis.

We have here stressed almost exclusively the emotional
dimension in gathering men and women into the Christian
church as it has been experienced within the Reformation
tradition. The importance of the emotional dimension in the
catholic tradition, both East and West, is so obvious and
overwhelming that its significance for the missionary ex-
pansion of these Christian traditions needs hardly any ex-
plication. Frequently people who have separated themselves
both cognitively and morally from these Christian communities have been kept enthralled by the emotional power
which overwhelmed all their intellectual scruples and moral
criticisms. Again, it seems strange that the historians of
Christianity have done so little for the investigation of the
emotional aspects of this movement, which, after all, was
born on Pentecost.

There is, however, also a fourth dimension of Christianity
which deserves our attention. It is the communal dimension
which involves us in relationships which identify, support,
and obligate us. In a pre-pluralistic society the question of
the community through which we identify ourselves hardly
comes up. The community to which we belong is evident
and natural. Practically everybody knows where he belongs,
knows who he is. In the pluralistic world, however, the
question of the community through which we identify ourselves becomes of crucial importance. We now have options.

We may use the political community, the national community, the racial community, the cultural community, the age community, and also the religious community for purposes of identification. The American sociologist, Will Herberg, pointed out years ago that for Americans the terms Protestant, Catholic, and Jew were largely means of sociological identification. He claimed that when a new family moved into a typical American suburban neighborhood and the question arose, "What are they?", the answer looked for was: Protestant, Catholic, or Jewish. In the religiously homogeneous districts of Europe or Asia this question and answer would make no sense at all. But as pluralization progresses the significance of the religious community as a focus of identification and discrimination increases. From the communal point of view, however, a person is what he accepts himself to be. The question is no longer, "What does he hold to be true?" or, "What does he consider right and wrong?" or even, "What are his religious feelings or experiences?", but rather, "What does he accept himself to be?", "With which community does he identify himself?" Here again the Jewish experience may be paradigmatic. The question, "Who is a Jew?" has never been answered to the satisfaction of Jews or non–Jews. At present, most Jews would be willing to grant that a Jew is a person who accepts himself as a Jew. The situation among Christians has become very similar. A Christian is a person who accepts himself as a member of this communion. All other human criteria have become ever more difficult to apply. And the same holds true for the confessional groups within Christianity. Who is a Roman Catholic? Who is a Protestant? The answer can hardly be given on the basis of cognitive, moral, or emotional criteria, because some people who believe, hold to be right, or feel what Roman Catholics are supposed to believe, hold to be right, or feel accept themselves as Protestants; and some people who believe, hold to be right, or feel what Protestants are supposed to believe, hold to be right, or feel accept themselves as Roman Catholics. And, what is even more shocking, increasingly many who believe, hold to be right, or feel nothing traditionally associated with one Christian confession or the other nevertheless consider themselves honestly to be members of the Christian community.

Thus in a pluralistic world, the communal aspect of Christianity has assumed great importance for many modern men and women, similar to the importance of this aspect for those who consider themselves Jews. Here again the Jewish experience as a minority in an alien world has anticipated the pluralistic development in which all religions experience themselves as minorities in a world in which the majority sees everything differently.

It would help us to understand the Christian task in a pluralistic world better if we realize that Christianity itself has a pluralistic character, has many dimensions—cognitive, moral, emotional, and communal—which will make a variety of contacts with other elements of this pluralistic world possible. Indeed, the pluralistic character of Christianity, here detailed, allows for the conscious utilization of all these dimensions for the interpretation of Christianity to modern man. We must no longer restrict ourselves to an exclusive emphasis on the cognitive or even moral elements. A Christian apologetics that starts with the logical demonstration of the existence of God is not helpful to people who are in need of the support which the emotional or communal dimensions of Christianity may be able to give them. Conversely, those who are troubled by intellectual doubts may indeed be helped by the theoretical discussion which addresses some of their cognitive concerns. In short, in a pluralistic world there can be no standard communication; it has to be varied and precise to meet the needs of the great variety of people with their complex and varied problems. But in this effort we shall soon discover that even the most sensitive and serious understanding of the various dimensions of Christianity will eventually reveal that God cannot be reached any more by emotion or community than by cognition or morality. These are indeed fascinating and very important dimensions of Christianity as religion and essential for its understanding. It has been a great mistake to neglect all but the cognitive aspect in our efforts to explain and communicate the Christian faith. But ultimately they reveal that there is no way from man to God, neither by reason or morality nor by emotion or community. The Gospel is God's reaching out to us, the people who are in darkness, and giving us his light. This encounter with the Gospel can happen as easily while we are becoming aware of the futility of our effort to achieve salvation through cognition as while we realize the ultimate inadequacy of our feelings or our morality. In the old theological categories of the Reformation, cognition, morality, emotion, and community are all ways in which we confront God's law and extremely important for the inescapable human task of world construction and world maintenance. Because theologians have so long neglected the emotional and communal aspects they have been of less help in this important human endeavor than a more ample understanding of the human situation might have made possible. Yet the proclamation of the Gospel in a pluralistic world means ultimately that the men and women engaged in the serious, exhilarating, and inescapable process of world construction and world maintenance must be allowed to experience again and again that in spite of the failures of our cognitive systems, our moral codes, our emotional experience and expressions, and our communal search for identity, God is with men; he has chosen to be with them in the midst of the failures and frustrations of their many reality-defining agencies. Precisely this is the Gospel in a pluralistic world, the good news: "For God sent not His Son into the world to condemn the world, but that the world through Him might be saved" (John 3:17).

II

VARIETIES

OF RELIGIOUS

COMMITMENT

In Webster's *New International Dictionary* the meaning of "commit" is defined as follows: "To give in trust; to put into charge or keeping; entrust; consign." The example given by the dictionary for this first meaning of "commit" is the fifth verse of the 37th Psalm, where we read in the King James version of the Bible: "Commit thy way unto the Lord; trust also in him; and he shall bring it to pass."

While this is probably the most profound sense in which we can speak of a religious commitment, it is my claim that most people actually are religiously committed. This commitment takes place on three levels. The first is almost universal; the second includes the vast majority of people; and only the third level of religious commitment is restricted to a minority—for reasons I shall point out later.

First, a few words about the first type of commitment. Here religious commitment is the acceptance of an historical–cultural tradition. A person identifies himself with a particular tradition and accepts it as his own. This religious tradition may be Hindu or Buddhist; it may be Zuni or Dobu. For Americans, it is generally Jewish or Christian. This commitment is a form of self–acceptance. It is the admission that this is the kind of man I am. These are my antecedents, this is my history, this is how I came to be who I am. It is, in a sense, a commitment to history. It does not have to be dishonest or uncritical. My citizenship in the

United States, for example, does not imply uncritical acceptance of everything American or carping depreciation of everything non–American, but simply facing the fact that I am who I am. My membership in the Forell family does not imply that my mother is the *only* good mother, but that she is *my* mother.

Religious commitment on this first level is very similar. I accept my religious past as part of my present, and I must admit, I accept it gratefully and proudly.

Since I am a Christian, I can best illustrate what this commitment means for Christians. First, it is a commitment to the church as the guardian and herald of these values. The church is the bridge to the past, yet at the same time involved in the fascinating effort to find new ways of expressing these values creatively in the present.

Second, it is a commitment to the Bible as the document which has shaped me and my people. It is the clue to Shakespeare as well as John Updike, to Goethe as well as Pär Lagerkvist, to Pascal as well as André Gide. If I don't know the Bible I cannot know myself. This book is important not only for what it meant at the time it was written, but also for what it has continued to mean in every age that followed, from the interpretations of the Rabbis of the Talmud to Bultmann and Barth in our time.

Third, it is a commitment to the validity of the religious experience. Even if I never shuddered in awe before the vastness of the universe and the beauty of holiness, commitment means that I shall respect such experiences in others and be sincerely grateful for them—just as I respect the painter and the composer and am grateful for them, though I may not be able to paint or compose.

This, then, is the first type of religious commitment; whether necessary or not, it is in fact more or less clearly part of the life of most Americans. It is a possible option for everybody; there is nothing supernatural about it; and, unlike many of my colleagues in the field of theology, I consider it desirable.

What about the second type of religious commitment? Here, religious commitment is the acceptance of a social–moral perspective. A person so committed asserts that, for him, religion and ethics belong together, and he gives assent in thought, word, and deed to the moral vision of his religion. It is, in a sense, a commitment to righteousness. While this is possible within the context of all major religions, I want to discuss it from the point of view of the Christian faith. First, it is a commitment to the church as a moral and maternal community that both teaches and upholds these values and helps her children to put them into practice. It is within the fellowship of this community, of which the family is the smallest and most important unit, that Christians learn what is right and wrong. In the context of the church, morality receives a dimension of significance that it does not have if it is approached from a merely prudential or rationalistic point of view.

Second, it is a commitment to the Bible as the "Good Book," as the saying goes. This popular expression reflects the ethical connotations which the Bible has for all those who read it in the light of this type of commitment. For them it is not merely history, but it has primarily an ethical message. This is the presupposition with which this book is read. Such readers are sometimes embarrassed by the fact that the Bible does not lend easily itself in all places to this approach. Nevertheless, that is the approach of this commitment. The Bible is the guide to the good life. Those passages that contain clear moral exhortations, like the Ten Commandments or the Sermon on the Mount or even I Corinthians 13 are the favorite passages of those committed in this second sense. "He has showed you, O man, what is good; and what does the Lord require of you but to do justice, and to love kindness, and to walk humbly with your

God?" (Mic. 6:8). They tend to read all of the Bible in the light of this moral vision.

Third, religious experience is seen as moral experience—summarized by Paul in the sentence, "Be not deceived, God is not mocked, what a man sows he shall also reap" (Gal. 6:7). Thus a man who has learned to live the good life in obedience to his conscience and in peace with his neighbors is the religious man in the vision of this type of commitment.

Such a religious commitment, while not quite as prevalent as the first type of commitment, nevertheless, is real to a majority of Americans. While they may not always live up to their ethical–religious vision, it guides many, even though they may at times be embarrassed by it and hesitate to admit it. It is the vision of the Law as Law of God and thus deeply rooted in almost all major religious traditions. It plays a dominant part in Judaism and Christianity. This, too, is a possible option for everybody. If it has supernatural overtones for most, it does not have them for all. It is quite possible to be authentically committed in this second sense without accepting any dogma of classical Christianity. Again, I would be prepared to say that I welcome such commitment, even though some theologians may disagree. So far as I can judge, such a commitment to righteousness is a most courageous, human, and desirable commitment, indeed.

But there is also a third kind of commitment. It is the acceptance of the revelation of the Absolute in a special form or even in a multitude of special forms. Lest we get side–tracked into the complexities of the comparative study of religion, let me try to illustrate the third type of commitment with the language of Christianity. For Christians, this commitment is the commitment to Jesus the Christ as the disclosure of the meaning, purpose, and ultimate destiny of each human life in the plan of God. To quote Paul again, it is a commitment to the proclamation that "God was in Christ reconciling the world unto himself" (II Cor. 5:19).

From this perspective, the church is the people of God, the body of Christ destined to bring mankind into fellowship with this Lord. The Bible is the cradle of Christ, proclaiming the faith of its writers in this Lord and through the power of God the Spirit, producing faith in those who are destined to hear. Religious experience is the encounter with the living God in the crucified Nazarene.

I have made my descriptions of this third type of commitment short because I really do not think that it is a commitment in the same sense as the other two types of commitment. One can volunteer for the first two commitments; I think one should. The third commitment is more like selective service; one is drafted. Within the tradition of classical Protestantism at least, it makes absolutely no sense to demand the third type of commitment from anybody. It is a gift of the Holy Spirit. Thus, it makes no sense to blame anybody for failing to be committed in the third sense, and it is actually obscene to take any credit for one's own commitment in this third sense.

While I would be willing to discuss what Christians have in fact meant by this third type of commitment, I consider it impossible for man to make it out of his own power. It is possible by grace alone.

On the other hand, the other types of commitment are viable options for everybody, and I would hope that all of us would give them serious consideration. They do not endanger your honesty or integrity; on the contrary, they allow you to face your historical and moral existence, in the words of the Bible to "honor your father and your mother, that your days may be long in the land which the Lord your God gives you."

But all of these commitments are related. While they are not equally available, the first two commitments rest ultimately upon the third commitment. It is because some people, at all times, have experienced the third type of commitment that the tradition of the first type of commitment and the ethics of the second type of commitment have developed. They are profoundly interrelated and by no means mutually exclusive. Perhaps they could be depicted as three concentric circles: the first commitment would be the largest outer circle, the second would be somewhat smaller, and the third would be the inner core.

Nevertheless, those of us who openly and unapologetically defend the reality of the third commitment are convinced that all those who take their stand on the other two commitments somehow belong to us, are part of us, and might eventually be brought into complete fellowship with us. Thus we believe that the first two commitments, which are open to everyone, are preparatory to the third commitment.

Actually the third commitment is not a commitment of man at all. It is rather the confession that God has committed himself to man, that he has accepted man, though man considers himself unacceptable. The third type of commitment is really, in the phrase of Paul Tillich, "to accept our acceptance, in spite of the fact that we are unacceptable," or in the ancient language of the church, "Justification by grace through faith."

III

CHRISTIAN
FREEDOM AND RELIGIOUS
LIBERTY

A theological investigation of the concept of religious liberty should begin with a look at the Bible. What does the Bible have to say on this subject? The answer is somewhat discouraging. The word "freedom" or "liberty" occurs only eight times in the Old Testament (*deror*) and twelve times in the New Testament (*eleutheria*). In the Old Testament it refers always to the kind of freedom slaves might obtain through the generosity of their masters. In the New Testament it is used only in the Epistles, and especially by the Apostle Paul, and describes the new stance of the child of God granted him by Christ.

Personal religious liberty as a civil right assumes a concept of the individual completely alien to the way in which both Old and New Testament writers think. It is as alien to them as nuclear physics or biochemistry.

Thus, if we want to achieve theological clarity on the subject of religious liberty we cannot rely on prooftexts from the Bible. We must rather try to see what the implications of the nature and destiny of man as proclaimed in the biblical witness are for the understanding of the religious liberty of men and women living in a pluralistic country and a pluralistic world.

In order to reduce the confusion we shall make an arbitrary distinction in this chapter between "Christian freedom" and "religious liberty." We shall use these terms in a specific and restricted sense.

"Christian freedom" is a theological term describing that gift of the Holy Spirit which the Apostle Paul calls *eleutheria* and which is translated variously in the New Testament as "liberty": ". . . because the creation itself will be set free from its bondage to decay and obtain the glorious liberty of the children of God" (Rom. 8:21); or "freedom": ". . . where the Spirit of the Lord is, there is freedom" (II Cor. 3:17); "For freedom Christ has set us free; stand fast therefore, and do not submit again to a yoke of slavery" (Gal. 5:1). Christian freedom is a gift of God which is not directly dependent upon the social or political status of the recipient. It may be present in prisoners or slaves and absent in rulers or princes. Its opposite is *douleia*—slavery to the law, death, and the demonic powers which constitute the bondage of the will.

"Religious liberty" is generally understood as one major aspect of civil liberty. The term "civil liberty" describes "the sum of the rights and immunities of all the citizens of an organized civil community concurrent with the guaranteed protection against interference with such rights and privileges."

It is rooted in the West in certain assumptions about the human race and man as typically expressed in the Declaration of Independence:

We hold these truths to be self–evident, that all men are created equal, that they are endowed by their creator with certain inalienable rights, that among these are life, liberty, and the pursuit of happiness. To secure these rights, governments are instituted among men, deriving their just powers from the consent of the governed.

Civil liberty is implemented by basic laws, of which the Bill of Rights of the United States Constitution is a significant example. To be effective, civil liberty depends upon the existence of an organized civil community, willing and able to enforce such laws. The disintegration of such a community into chaos is as real a threat to civil liberty as the establishment of a tyrannical government which openly flouts civil, political, individual, and personal liberty.

For the Christian, all civil liberties are rooted in the fact that man is created by God for fellowship with him. He must defend these liberties because of his understanding of the human situation and his vision of the ultimate destiny of man.

To be sure, "religious liberty" is a political term and as such is not dependent upon Christian freedom. It is the inherent right of the human race and of each person to worship or not worship God or the gods. It provides that nobody be prevented from worship or compelled to worship. Religious liberty involves the right to form religious associations for the purpose of common worship and the right of religious assembly. It also implies a right to change one's religion. The religious liberty of any individual or group, however, is limited by the liberty of other individuals and groups. My right to promote my faith does not grant me the right to make anybody listen to me who does not want to listen. My right to abstain from all worship does not give me the right to prevent others from worshiping if they so desire.

Religious liberty, although according to most American Protestants the inalienable right of all men, is actually a fairly recent and tenuous political achievement. It is constantly threatened by the actual or imagined need for a universally accepted religious foundation for the political community. In the modern world this religious foundation is not only sought among the great "world religions" but particularly among the "pseudo-religions"—Marxism, biologism, racism, and statism[1]—whose totalitarian claims represent the most acute threat to religious liberty.

[1] Joachim Wach, *The Comparative Study of Religion* (New York: Columbia University Press, 1958), pp. 37–38.

CHRISTIAN FREEDOM:
ITS NATURE AND CONSEQUENCES

Christian freedom as a possession of men is the result of the deed of God in Christ on the cross. "Truly, truly, I say to you, everyone who commits sin is a slave to sin. The slave does not continue in the house forever; the son continues forever. So if the Son makes you free, you will be free indeed" (John 8:34–36). The truth that makes men free and makes them children of God is not information about the universe or man or about the arts and sciences, important as all these truths may be, but the good news (gospel) that in Jesus, the Christ, God has overcome the powers that enslave man: law, death, and the demonic principalities.

This victory of God on man's behalf is not some esoteric piece of information without significance for the daily life of man, but it enables him to walk in newness of life. "We are buried therefore with him by baptism into death, so that as Christ was raised from the dead by the glory of the Father, we too might walk in newness of life" (Rom. 6:4). Thus the victory has direct consequences for the Christian's understanding of his opportunities and obligations in the various civil communities.

Bondage of the Law

Christian freedom as a divine gift reorients man in relation to the law. Because the fact of law confronts man in the structures of his environment and in the codes of his society, all men experience themselves as circumscribed and limited. The law makes it obvious that they live in a world not of their own making, surrounded by structures which have been formulated by other men at other times, and which restrain and obstruct the individual's wishes.

As a result, the law is experienced as a limitation. Men will devise ways of circumventing the law by obeying its letter while ignoring its underlying content. This "legalism," an obsession with the letter which obscures the spirit, was scorned by Jesus in his controversy with the legalists of his time. It was in this context that he proclaimed that the Sabbath was made for man, and not man for the Sabbath. Christian freedom transforms the law from a threatening imperative to an indicative which describes for him the new possibilities of the children of God to live lives of gratitude and love. The Christian knows that love is the fulfillment of the law and is no longer concerned with the letter but rather the spirit. From a fence which obstructs his wishes it becomes for the believer a description of the possibilities of a life of love and service.

Bondage of Death

Christian freedom as a divine gift reorients man in relation to death. The fact that all men must die and that consciously or unconsciously they are always aware of it produces the "anxiety of death" which "overshadows all concrete anxieties and gives them their ultimate seriousness."[2]

The attempt of man to ignore death and remove it from all serious and conscious consideration produces the pathetic efforts to attain eternal youth by biochemical, psychological, or surgical devices. The obsession with death expresses itself on the one hand in the vain effort to remain eternally young. On the other hand, and on a more sophisticated level, the reality of death may be openly faced, and this may produce a death-obsession such as is reflected in the literature that is completely death-centered and in which the knowledge of death tomorrow has destroyed all meaning of life today.

Christian freedom—the result of being partakers of Christ's victory over death—enables man to live today with-

[2] Paul Tillich, *The Courage to Be* (New Haven: Yale University Press, 1952), p. 43.

out constant anxiety about tomorrow. It frees man from obsession with death for the new life of discipleship in obedience to Christ.

Bondage to Demonic Principalities

Christian freedom as a divine gift liberates man from the demonic principalities which threaten him daily. Modern man experiences these demonic principalities in the impersonal forces that hold him in subjection and try to depersonalize him and reduce him from a child of God to a numbered robot. They are mainly of two types: hereditary and environmental.

Hereditary enslavement results from obsession with race, nationality, and sex. Modern man is often only a faceless and heartless representative of his race, his nationality, and his sex. He derives all his significance from his participation in these collectivities.

Environmental enslavement results from the state, the class, the caste, economic power, and political power. Here man is merely citizen of proletarian, lower middle-class, or capitalist society, voter or office–seeker. But man as "economic man" or "political animal" is far less than a human person. Christ's victory over the demonic powers as they confront modern man frees man from the tyranny and idolatry of these abstractions for a life of freedom where the interest of the person for whom Christ died is in the center.

Historical and Eschatological Dimensions

Christian freedom as a divine gift also has historical and eschatological dimensions. It is man's possession because it has been achieved by God's deed in Christ *sub Pontio Pilato*. It is not a freedom which he may achieve through his own striving, but rather a freedom which is available to him when he accepts the good news that he has in fact been freed out of the bondage of his slavery. But while the liberation is an accomplished fact, it points to the future, the realization and fulfillment of all freedom in the coming kingdom of God. The Christian's life of freedom in the various cultural communities of which he is a part is a life in which faith in the accomplished fact (cross and resurrection) and hope of the coming kingdom (*parousia*) must again and again be expressed in deeds of love. The Christian is called to a life of parabolic action, that is, a life in which he serves Christ in the neighbor, in fellowship with the entire communion of believers, hoping his deeds of love, empowered by Jesus Christ, may be used by the Holy Spirit to point men to the Father.

HUMAN RIGHTS: IDEAL AND REALITY

The ontological root of all human rights, and especially of religious liberty, is the creation of man in the image of God. It is because man is a creature who is created for conversation with God, to whom God speaks and who is called to respond (who is responsible), that these rights are inalienable. Their alienation affects man's humanity. It dehumanizes him.

The existential root of man's dehumanization is sin— man's revolt against God—which jeopardizes his humanity, his "life, liberty, and pursuit of happiness." Because of sin man is his own worst enemy. He who is created "responsible" becomes "irresponsible."

Because of the contradiction between man as God's creature (Gen. 1:26) created in God's image, and proud and unbelieving man in revolt against his creator (Gen. 3:1), there exists a permanent and dynamic tension between the *ideal* of human rights and their *reality*. The ideal of human rights is rooted in the notion of "true law as right reason in agreement with nature."[3] This concept of "natural law" as

3 Cicero, *De Re Publica*, II, pp. 22, 23.

available to all men, while not original with Christianity, is the common property of all major Christian traditions. For Aquinas "the natural law is nothing else than the rational creature's participation of the eternal law."[4] Luther said, "All men have a certain natural knowledge implanted in their minds whereby they naturally perceived that they ought to do unto others as they would have others do unto them. This proposition and others like it we call natural law, and they are the foundation of human justice and of all good works."[5] Similarly, Calvin said, "It is certain that the natural law of God, which we call the moral law, is no other than a declaration of natural law and of that conscience which has been engraven by God on the minds of men; the whole rule of this equity, of which we now speak, is prescribed in it."[6]

Yet, while there may be unanimity about the existence of such a natural law, the exact content is the subject of an on-going debate. It is discovered and defined by the aid of reason. While, at times, this has been understood to mean that an exact code of "natural law" can be deduced from man's rationality, many contemporary advocates of "natural law" would proceed in a more cautious and empirical fashion and say, "There are panhuman universals as regards needs and capacities that shape, or could at least rightly shape, the broad outlines of a morality that transcends cultural differences."[7] As the same author has stated in another place, "The two most vast empirical generalizations that can be made about *homo sapiens* are that he is a symbol-using animal and an evaluating animal. These generalizations are intimately related and they transcend all cultural

---

[4] Thomas Aquinas, *Summa Theologica*, Q. 91, art. 2.

[5] Martin Luther, *W.A.*, 40, II, p. 66.

[6] John Calvin, *Institutes*, IV, Book IV, Chap. XX, Sec. 16.

[7] Clyde Kluckhohn, *Culture and Behavior* (New York: Macmillan, 1962), p. 270.

differences. . . . All cultures have had their categorical imperatives that went beyond existence and pleasure."[8]

The fact that such categorical imperatives are discovered and defined by the aid of reason involves them in the theological problem of reason. Reason is for the Christian a God–given tool enabling man to find viable standards for the solution for many of the problems that face him in his life on earth. Yet this same reason is used in the process of rationalization to pervert these standards to the advantage of those in power. This complexity and ambiguity of reason is thus reflected in the "natural law" it discovers.

Nevertheless, the notion of some form of universal right is implicit in any concept of "natural law." But these very rights depend for their realization upon specific and detailed positive laws. For example, the idea of the equality of man may be inherent in the nature of man. "We hold these truths to be self–evident, that all men are created equal," was the assertion of the Declaration of Independence. It merely echoed Cicero's statement, "No single thing is so like another, so exactly like its counterpart, as all of us are to one another. Nay, if bad habits and false beliefs did not twist the weaker minds and turn them in whatever direction they are inclined, no one would be so like his own self as all men would be like all others."[9] Yet this basic conviction from the grounds of reason and natural law that all men are inherently equal did not stop Jefferson or Cicero from owning slaves. This "ideal" equality became "real" only through the implementation of natural law by positive law. It was not the Declaration of Independence, but the Thirteenth and Fourteenth Amendments to the Constitution of the United States and their enforcement which brought an end to slavery in America.

[8] *Ibid.*, p. 334.
[9] Cicero, *De Legibus I*, X, p. 29.

Because of the tension between man created in God's image and man in revolt against his Creator, the idea of natural law and of the human rights derived therefrom is impotent unless it is ever and again enacted in positive laws which are enforced by the organized civil community. At the same time the positive laws thus enforced are bound to become unjust, tyrannical, or irrelevant unless they are constantly re–examined in the light of the principles of natural law which they are designed to realize.

Whenever the Christian church sees its message in regard to the civil order exclusively in the light of Genesis 1:26, the divine image in man, it underestimates the reality of sin, and its influence is negated by sentimental naivete. Conversely, whenever the church's message is determined exclusively by Genesis 3:1 ff., the fall of man, it underestimates the human possibilities given to the first Adam and restored by the second Adam, and its influence is negated by harsh legalism.

Attainment and Protection of Human Rights in the Civil Community

Human rights and freedoms have their origin in the divinely ordered nature of man and the divinely ordered function of the human community. It is because of the destiny of man in God's purpose that he has rights potentially. It is because of the proper operation of the community in which he happens to live that he may have these rights actually.

The actual operation of the civil community is of crucial importance to the realization of the rights and freedoms of its members. It is by developing a properly functioning and adjustable design that they are procured and preserved.

The Christian church has no ideological concern in the nature of the civil community, but rather a practical concern with its functioning. It has no "model state" derived from Scripture or reason or a combination of both which it can offer for imitation or adoption. Political mythologies ranging from the "divine right of kings" to the "infallibility of the general will" and from "conservatism" to "liberalism" must be judged on the basis of their functional efficiency in the interest of human persons. They are tolerable as long and insofar as they safeguard concrete and personal human rights and liberties; they are dangerous idols if the theoretical justice they proclaim obscures the practical injustice they produce.

But this very absence of an ideological political commitment on the part of the church does imply a preference for those "open societies" where there is room for politically uncommitted people whose ultimate concern is not the state or even society. The church will favor social arrangements which supply correctives to the dangers which the apotheosis of "liberty" or "welfare" or other abstractions of this kind might produce. Because of the availability of correctives to excesses in a properly functioning democratic society, such a society will generally contribute most to the attainment and protection of human rights.

The church will contribute most to the attainment and preservation of the maximum of personal and human rights and liberties by concerning itself primarily with the operation rather than the ideology of civil and political communities. Human rights and liberties are a matter of action rather than invocation, and it is much more difficult but much more fruitful to design and operate the open and adjustable political machinery which makes them possible than to write manifestoes favoring good and opposing evil in general.

In the practical application of these insights it will become apparent that attainment of human rights is the result of two factors: the positive recognition of these rights as due to others; and the negative fear of the eventual loss of our own rights when the rights of the neighbor are jeopardized. It seems apparent that while the first factor has great theoretical force, it is the second factor that produces action. For example, it was the evolving religious pluralism in America as much as any theories about religious liberty which produced the religious liberty Americans actually enjoy. Men will more easily grant liberties to others if they can be shown that not doing so will jeopardize their own.

Relations Between Christian Freedom, Religious Liberty, and Civil Liberties

Christian freedom, the gift of God's grace, frees the Christian from the bondage of the idols which are threatened by religious liberty and civil liberties, and thus empowers him to give himself freely to the task of helping all men attain those liberties which are within reach of all men.

As long as my religion is an achievement which is threatened by the existence of other religions, I am forced to overcome this threat to my salvation by fanaticism and the persecution of the "infidel" who jeopardizes my religious existence by his existence. Religious persecution and the failure to grant religious liberty is often the result of man's inability to overcome his own doubts in faith. He externalizes the conflict by persecuting his own doubts in the person who does not believe as he does. The divine act which frees man from the slavery of sin also frees him from fanaticism and hate for sympathy and love.

Whenever religion is used as a mythological integrating principle of a socio–political community, religious liberty is considered a threat to stability. This is the basis of all religious persecutions initiated by the political authorities from the persecution of Socrates to that of the Jehovah's Witnesses. The insistence on a minimum of religious agreement within the commonwealth, which has dominated Western thought from Constantine to John Dewey, is essentially a political concern. This does not mean that such a "public philosophy" may not in fact be an essential aspect of an orderly society, but as such it is the concern of all citizens, whatever their religion. It was Voltaire, no friend of the Christian faith, who said, "If there were no God it would be necessary to invent him." But while the "invented God" of the "public philosophy," like the "royal lie" of Plato, may be a political necessity, such a "god" is an idol in the light of Christian freedom. The confusion of the "public philosophy" with the Christian faith is a dangerous threat to the latter's integrity.

Christian freedom releases men from bondage to all political mythologies and other absolute loyalties. For it is God alone who deserves such complete devotion. But this sovereign desires that men should trust and love him without compulsion. He is unwilling to force any man into fellowship with himself. It is the assertion of the Christian faith that man may resist God's seeking love for time and eternity. But if the all–wise and almighty God refuses to force his will on man, even though such exertion of force might be in man's best interest, it is a blasphemous usurpation of God's place if man tries to use force to crush religious resistance and obtain conformity. It is this reflection which makes respect for the religious liberty of others not only a demand of civil justice but a necessary implication of the Christian faith.

The relation of Christian freedom to other liberties and rights is similar to its relation to religious liberty. Man is unwilling to grant rights to others because of his idolization of the principalities and powers whose rule these liberties threaten. It is because of the idolization of my "race" that the freedoms of other races are reduced. It is because of the threat to my group's political and economic idols that the freedom of those who oppose them is abrogated. And the uncritical and idolatrous deification of my religious institutions makes me demand the suppression or even extermination of all religious institutions which differ from my own. Christian freedom, by releasing man from all false gods, obviates the necessity of defending these idols at the cost of the rights and liberties of other men. Since salvation is not racial, national, political, economic, or even "religious," the ultimate devotion to these causes is unmasked as idolatrous worship of false gods, and man is freed from idolatry for the service of the person of the neighbor. He is freed from serving the "Sabbath" to serving man. This does not, however, produce some abstract list of "liberties" and "rights" which the Christian is bound to advocate and defend at all costs; but, rather, frees him to love his neighbor and to evaluate all "rights" and "liberties" in the light of their concrete and functional significance for real human persons.

Christian Faith and Civil Authority

According to the Bible, civil authority is ordering power, having its origin in God. Thus a Christian understanding of government must see it in relation to the creative and preserving will of God. The state, in whatever form it may appear, is never directly and immediately of the "order of creation" in the particular manner in which it happens to organize the community. But the power which expresses itself in all civil authorities is of God. This power can be used or abused, and the evaluation of any civil authority must be on the grounds of its proper use of power on behalf of man.

The confusion of the issue comes when authority is explained in terms of its *origin* according to some political theory rather than in terms of its function. Then the legitimacy of authority becomes dependent upon an abstract theory concerning its past. All efforts to prove the legitimacy of royal, republican, or dictatorial authority on the basis of its origin in a social contract or a proletarian revolution are hopelessly beside the point. Not only do they not prove anything—for Hobbes, Locke, Rousseau, and Marx could justify all sorts of empirical states from the same basic principles—but they detract from the true criterion of civil authority, namely, does it fulfill the task for which it was created?

It is its mission to establish "civil justice" or, in biblical terms, to be "not a terror to good conduct, but to bad" (Rom. 13:3); "to punish those who do wrong and to praise those who do right" (I Pet. 2:14). The criterion for the evaluation of the legality of civil authority is not to be found in an analysis of its historical origin or the intention of its constitution or the moral standards of the individuals who happen to occupy positions of power. The justification of civil authority lies in the fulfillment of its divinely ordered function on behalf of man.

Civil authority, as human authority, is subject to all the frailties of man and thus is in need of help and criticism. It must be understood that its function is good and that the criterion by which it is to be judged is the service it renders to the earthly welfare of human persons in their life together and as individuals. The tendency to condemn all authority and power as inherently evil is most dangerous for the life and welfare of man. For, as the exercise of authority is important for the survival of humanity at all times and all places, it becomes indispensable in the highly complex modern technological society. Undisciplined behavior in traffic may have been annoying when the means of transportation was donkeys and camels. It is fatal when the means of transportation is high–powered automobiles and supersonic jets. The depreciation of authority can have the most dangerous consequences. For example, the disappearance of civil authority from the core of our metropolitan population centers results in a jungle which tends to destroy humans utterly. Thus, many of our most flagrant social disorders are the result of the failure of civil authority to function responsibly and authoritatively.

Fair, equitable, and prompt law enforcement, which is possible only when civil authority operates properly, is one of the major conditions for the survival of human civilization. No form of government is more dependent upon authority than democracy. The fact that authority is more diffused and internalized does not detract from its obligatory nature. Civil authority is essential for good government everywhere, and "due process of law" is possible only within the framework of authority.

To assume that any civil liberty can be maintained while civil authority disintegrates is naive and contrary to all experience. In fact, the existence of civil liberty assumes stability and order which is invariably the by–product of civil authority, and the disintegration of civil authority is followed of necessity by the disappearance of all civil liberties. The eclipse of civil authority does not produce liberties, but rather subverts them and results in the tyranny of outlaws and gangsters.

Because of the Christian concern for the proper functioning of civil authority on behalf of the earthly welfare of humans, Christians are obliged to strengthen and support all those authorities which in fact maintain the liberty and welfare of all people in a just and equitable manner. This is not necessarily all "legitimate" authority, since this definition puts the stress on the moot question of the origin of civil authority. The Christian concern is with the just and equitable operation of civil authority on behalf of man, and only in a very secondary way with its origin. Since "there is no authority except from God" (Rom. 13:1), the question of origin is not theologically significant.

Civil authority as exercised by man is a natural and dangerous focus of demonic perversion. In the language of the Book of Revelation it can be that beast "with ten horns and seven heads" (Rev. 13:1). It is the characteristic of demonic civil authority that it is not satisfied with functioning on behalf of man but makes absolute ideological claims. Not satisfied to govern, it wants to save. Not satisfied to promote the earthly welfare of man, it promises him eternal happiness.

Against this demonic perversion of civil authority the church must speak its prophetic protest. "Here is a call for the endurance and faith of the saints" (Rev. 13:10). But it is important that the protest be made because of the ideological pretensions of civil authority and not because of disagreement about economic theory or political science. Christians can disagree with one another and with the civil authorities about economic and political theories. This is a place for constructive debate and criticism but not for prophetic protest. Christians as Christians do not necessarily have better insights into questions of geology or biology. There is no such thing as "Christian economics" or "Christian politics" or "Christian biology," but there are Christians engaged in economics and politics and biology. Only when the question of ultimate loyalty is raised must the Christian reply that he has to obey God rather than man. This cannot be the catch–all answer that supplies a convenient halo for one's political and economic idiosyncracies. It is reserved for the encounter with the "beast."

Religious Liberty as a Common Concern of Church and State

It is implicit in the nature of true government that its power should be exercised for the establishment and maintenance of justice. Such exercise of power is a check against the ever-present danger of chaos. At the same time, the rights of citizens must be jealously guarded since they, in turn, check the ever-present tendency to abuse of power and resulting tyranny.

The Christian community has the responsibility to support both aspects of this effort wherever possible. This is the more necessary since the Christian view of the human situation sees the just administration of the state and the right of the citizen constantly threatened by the political results of man's sin. Thus, power has a corrupting tendency in the hands of men, and government by law is to be preferred to government by men. It is awareness of the pervasiveness of human sin which makes Christians welcome a system of checks and balances as incorporated in constitutional democracies. Insistence on "due process of law" in the operation of government tends to protect the individual person against the whims of the powerful, be they individuals or majorities.

In the exercise of this responsibility the Christian church has the right and the duty to speak up and to provide an open and fair forum for the discussion of the controversial issues debated.

When the church in convention or through its chosen leaders speaks, it does not claim infallibility but the right to contribute a point of view, informed by the Christian perspective, to the issues being debated. To silence the Christian church on all controversial issues because of the obvious tension which such participation causes would rob a community of a sensitive and informed voice where such a voice is most needed. For the church's religious liberty means also the obligation to speak up on controversial issues through appropriate spokesmen even at the risk of offending those who hold differing views inside or outside of its own ranks.

But even more important is the church's task of providing an umbrella of faith under which people who disagree profoundly on matters of public policy can debate the issues and perhaps even reconcile their differences. Religious liberty for the church means that it can supply such opportunities for confrontation as part of its life and as an essential contribution to the development of democratic consensus in a pluralistic society. If the church does not exercise its liberty and make its facilities available for the discussion of the great topics of the time it dooms itself to irrelevancy and deprives the entire community of one of the most auspicious arenas for the debate of these issues.

Governmental authority can and should establish civil justice and liberty and thus promote the general welfare. The modern state has assumed many functions which at one time were assigned to the larger family. It has now a far more constructive and complex task than merely using the "sword" against criminals and aggressors. Even if it were desirable to reverse this process, such is not possible in the urban, industrial, and interdependent society in which we live. Thus the state has inherited the responsibility to guarantee equality of opportunity for all citizens in order to enable them to develop their God–given talents for their personal growth and the benefit of the common good. It is evident that minority groups, and especially the economically weak among them, are in need of governmental assistance and protection in order to assure equality of opportunity in political participation, education, free access to public services and facilities, employment, and housing. The modern state is the only agency available to safeguard these rights for all citizens. It is the task of the Christian community to support the efforts of the political community in its search for justice.

But what is the significance of the institutional forms of the church for its effectiveness in the proclamation of Christian freedom and its advocacy of civil liberty? The biblical witness does not supply a "model constitution" for the Christian church. In the course of the history of Christendom different patterns have been adopted, modified, and discarded. The relationship to civil authorities has been a significant factor in all of these patterns. The conviction that one must obey God rather than man has been part of each pattern, even though the critical point where this conflict must arise has been seen quite differently at different times. At all times, and while various patterns were in operation, Christians have been called to say in the face of powerful civil authorities, "Here I stand, I cannot do otherwise." From John Chrysostom, who proclaimed God's Word in the state–church of Byzantium and died in exile, to Bernard of Clairvaux, who criticized popes at the zenith of their power, to Luther and Calvin, Menno Simons and Roger Williams, the independence of the church has been the result largely of her obedience to the Word rather than of the pattern of her relationship to the civil government. Each such pattern has produced its own subtle temptations to those who relied on its effectiveness and their own powers to use it and thus become weak and unfaithful. It is just as easy to betray the Gospel to a powerful and perverse board of trustees close at hand as it is to a powerful and perverse king far away.

To assume that a particular administrative relationship to the civil authorities is a mark of the church and a guarantee of its faithfulness is naive and dangerous. It is equally dangerous to focus one's attention on the problem of the relationship to civil authority of people who lived at other times or in other parts of the world. Though these problems may be very real, they tend to draw our attention away from our own problems.

The principle of voluntarism and a church independent of the control of civil authorities has served Christians in the United States well. It has its own serious temptations which have produced a large literature. There is no solution in this world which does not have its own difficulties. These remain as a reminder that Christian freedom is a gift which man holds as a down-payment. The church as God's pilgrim people cannot see in any of its tent cities the heavenly

Jerusalem. Some of these temporary encampments may be better, some may be worse, but all are reminders that "here we have no lasting city, but we seek the city which is to come" (Heb. 13:14).

> For we know that if the earthly tent we live in is destroyed, we have a building from God, a house not made with hands, eternal in the heavens. Here indeed we groan, and long to put on our heavenly dwelling. . . . For while we are still in this tent, we sigh with anxiety; not that we would be unclothed, but that we would be further clothed, so that what is mortal may be swallowed up by life. He who has prepared us for this very thing is God, who has given us the Spirit as a guarantee. (II Cor. 5:1-5)

IV

GOD IS

DEAD?

About the so-called "God is dead" movement, one thing, and one thing alone, is clear: it is news. Like the ancient journalistic definition that dog bites man is not news, but man bites dog is news, the theologian claiming that God is dead can be sure of making headlines in the mass media.

But beyond this incontrovertible fact, what else can be said on the subject? As a professional investigator of the history of Christian thought, I would tend to ask of this theological school what I ask of Origen or Anselm, Thomas or Luther, Schleiermacher or Barth: What is the doctrinal intention behind the doctrinal form of the phrase "God is dead?" When the Apostles' Creed states that Jesus Christ "sitteth on the right hand of the Father," this statement is literally nonsense. Nobody ever believed that Christ sits *on* the right hand of the Father—although some may have had a fairly literal notion of his sitting *at* the right hand of the Father—but the task of the theologian is to discover the intent behind the form.

What do we do then, with the phrase "God is dead"? Literally this statement is nonsense. It is in the same class with the statement that this triangle has four angles. Implicit in the word "God" as used in Western civilization since the time of the Greeks is the attribute of immortality. You can deny that there is a God, but to say "God is dead" is the same as to say, "At one time there was an immortal God who has now died." And this is sheer nonsense. Unfortunately, some of the representatives of this movement have said things like, "God's death is an event in our history." I consider this kind of speech very confusing.

But the statement could also mean that the way in which some people have thought about God has become obsolete, and this popular image has died. This is, I suppose, the burden of J. A. T. Robinson's *Honest to God.* He believes that many people, until very recently, thought of God as sitting on a golden throne; most people today find this kind of imagery impossible. Thus, the God of their childish imagination is no more; he is dead.

If this is the message of the "God is dead" theologians, it would be my claim that this point is trivial. It may be very true that some Russian peasants were upset that the cosmonauts did not discover God and his heaven while circling the earth. But for most people and for all theologians in the history of Christendom, God was always omnipresent and his *immensitas* is part of every text book of dogmatics. Perhaps a quotation from St. Augustine's *Confessions* will illustrate this awe before the mystery of God which characterizes the classic Christian faith: "Since, then, Thou fillest heaven and earth, do they contain Thee? Or, as they contain Thee not, dost Thou fill them, and yet there remains something over? And where dost Thou pour forth that which remaineth of Thee when the heaven and earth are filled?"

This is as little the God "up there" as any description of God in Clement of Alexandria or John of Damascus.

If the "God is dead" movement is trying to tell us that the God of the childish imagination is not an adequate expression of the Christian faith, the observation is trivial and not theologically serious. Indeed, the entire sacramental theology of the Christian church is an eloquent denial of any geographical localization of God.

But there is a third possibility. Perhaps the "God is dead" prophets are trying to tell us that we do not need God any longer because modern science and technology have made man independent of such support as God may have given mankind in the past.

This, it seems to me, was the thrust of Professor Hamilton's article in *Theology Today*. He saw such hope in the technological advances of our age, the optimism of the civil rights movement, and last but by no means least the music of the Beatles, that he felt that while God died in heaven, all's right with the world.

Reading Professor Hamilton's article, and, earlier, Professor Cox's book *The Secular City*, a typically modest effort to update St. Augustine's *City of God*, I have the uncanny feeling that these men and I do not live in the same world. Perhaps this all–pervasive optimism has not reached us in Iowa, but my recent reading does not convince me that this mood of optimism is all–pervasive.

I was also struck by the fact that Professor Hamilton used Saul Bellow's *Herzog* as an example of this new mood. I read the book, but I could not say that it struck me as a very optimistic statement. Neither does the *Autobiography of Malcolm X* or *Manchild in the Promised Land* or even the report of the hearings on Viet Nam before the Senate Foreign Relations Committee.

Such optimism seems simply naive. To build a theology on such a misreading of the contemporary situation seems dangerous and foolish. History neither dooms nor redeems us. Any theology which is either optimistic or pessimistic obscures the real personal responsibility which we all have for our life. We cannot rely on the redemptive character of history unless we are Marxists or fools.

But perhaps I am quite wrong and the "God is dead" movement is neither nonsense nor trivial nor even naive, but rather the effort of some desperate men who were trained to be theologians but who lost their religion somewhere along the line to stay within the warm bosom of the church. Their stance, "There is no God, but Jesus is his Son," while not intellectually persausive, is not really so different from the description of the theological position attributed to George Santayana, "There is no God, and Mary is his mother."

Perhaps they are not quite ready for the cold, cruel world of atheism and seek the shelter of the community of Christian people against its stormy blasts. Thus they stay in Methodist universities and Baptist theological seminaries, not quite ready to live where some of us have to live and want to live, with atheists who do not love Jesus.

People frequently have lost faith in the history of religion. If faith is a gift of the Holy Spirit as Christians claim, such loss of faith is not blameworthy. Such people ought to be pitied rather than censured.

But this does not mean that just because they have lost their faith they have the right to speak for all Christians— as they frequently try to do—or that it gives them the right to interpret the Christian faith authoritatively. They should quietly fade away.

If you have followed me so far, you may wonder why I am willing to spend so much time on a movement which I have described as either nonsense, trivial, naive, or pathetic. The reason is simple. I believe that this discussion, the concern with the so–called "God is dead" movement, tends to confuse the serious issues which confront the Christian church and all men of good will in our time.

The issue is not the death of God but rather the death of man. As Erich Fromm has pointed out, the death of God was a nineteenth-century problem. It is the ripe fruit of romanticism as so profoundly expressed in Nietzsche's *Thus Spake Zarathustra*. But our problem today is the death of man. Since the sixteenth century, man has constantly lost significance. First Copernicus removed him from the center of the cosmic stage to some minor planet circling a minor star. Then Darwin took man and brought him into such close proximity to the animals that "man as the measure of all things" has become a statement increasingly obsolete, and the "ape as the measure of all things" would seem more accurate. Then Freud proceeded to show that the former "master of his soul and captain of his fate" is actually determined by a vast subconscious over which he has no control. It is not surprising, but significant, that one of the most popular books with teenagers was at one time *Robinson Crusoe*; it is now *Lord of the Flies*. This book is a consistent bestseller among high school students. Defoe believed that man could conquer the wilderness and make the desert bloom. Golding tells us that civilization is a strange interlude and the beast will conquer.

The abolition of man as man, so deeply felt by the person who sees himself as a social security number on an IBM card or a computer tape, is the problem of our time. The mood expressed in *Last Exit to Brooklyn* is not a mood manufactured by theologians but rather by some of the most sensitive spirits of the age.

The Fire Next Time is hardly a very optimistic statement about the inescapable progress of man. In the latter part of the twentieth century, the main problem of man is man. We know now, or soon will know, how we can design the new man. We will have the technical skill to remake him; just as we have the technical skill now to kill every man on this earth.

The problem is not technology, but how we are going to use our vast powers? Right now we use them to bomb and destroy men, women, and children.

This then is our problem: "Who is man that Thou art mindful of him?" It seems to this observer that the death-of-God movement is "sand in the eyes." It wastes time on the wrong question. It is also my conviction that cutting man off from God makes the solution to this problem even more difficult.

It seems that man is man in relationship to God and the neighbor. Whenever the relationship to God is destroyed the relationship to the neighbor seems to suffer as well.

It is for this reason that I would hope Christian theologians, as well as all other people interested in the earthly welfare of man, would forget the debate about the death of God. God is not dependent on our approval, support, or even belief. Let us rather concentrate on the question how we can prevent the death of man "before the night cometh when no man can work."

V

THE ILLUSION
OF NEUTRALITY

In the animated discussion concerning the place of God and religion in the public schools, the term that has received a good deal of approbation as describing the proper stance of the state—and the public school as an agency of the state—in relationship to religion is the term neutrality.

It is this word which is used again and again by the Supreme Court to set forth what it considers the constitutional attitude toward this problem. In the famous Schemp case, Justice Clark cites with approval the opinion of Judge Alphonso Taft, who said almost one hundred years ago that in regard to religion "the government is neutral, and while protecting all, it prefers none, and it disparages none."[1] Later, the same opinion continues: "The wholesome 'neutrality' of which this Court's cases speak thus stems from a recognition of the teachings of history that powerful sects or groups might bring about a fusion of governmental and religious functions or a concert or dependency of one upon the other and to the end that official support of the state or federal government would be placed behind the tenets of one or of all orthodoxies. This the Establishment Clause prohibits. And a further reason for neutrality is found in the Free Exercise Clause, which recognizes the value of religious training, teaching and observance, and, more particularly, the right of every person to freely choose his own

[1] Frommer, *The Bible and the Public Schools* (New York: A Liberal Press Book, 1963), p. 67.

47

course with reference thereto, free of any compulsion from the state. This the Free Exercise Clause guarantees."[2]

Toward the very end, the opinion states again, "In the relationship between man and religion, the State is firmly committed to a position of neutrality."[3]

Again in the concurring opinion of Justice Brennan we read: ". . . The First Amendment commands not official hostility toward religion, but only a strict neutrality in matters of religion."[4] And he continues later, "The state must be steadfastly neutral in all matters of faith, and neither favor nor inhibit religion."[5]

Justice Goldberg, in his concurring opinion, takes up the problem of neutrality also and deals with it in the following paragraph: "It is said, and I agree, that the attitude of the state toward religion must be one of neutrality. But untutored devotion to the concept of neutrality can lead to invocation or approval of results which partake not simply of that non-interference and noninvolvement with the religious which the Constitution commands, but of a brooding and pervasive devotion to the secular and a passive or even active hostility to the religious. Such results are not only not compelled by the Constitution, but, it seems to me, are prohibited by it."[6]

Also in the dissenting opinion of Justice Stewart, the concept of neutrality is discussed. He writes: "For a compulsory state educational system so structures a child's life that if religious exercises are held to be impermissible activity in schools, religion is placed at an artificial and state–created disadvantage. Viewed in this light, permission of such exercises for those who want them is necessary if the schools

[2] *Ibid.*, p. 74 f.
[3] *Ibid.*, p. 79.
[4] *Ibid.*, p. 152.
[5] *Ibid.*, p. 155.
[6] *Ibid.*, p. 164.

are truly to be neutral in the matter of religion. And a refusal to permit religious exercises thus is seen, not as the realization of state neutrality, but rather as the establishment of a religion of secularism, or at the least, as government support of the beliefs of those who think that religious exercises should be conducted only in private."[7]

In view of the significance which the term "neutrality" has acquired in the discussion of religion and the public schools, it may be of some help to discuss the precise meaning of the term and its possible implications.

Neutrality, according to the dictionary, is the "condition of being uninvolved in contests or controversies between others; the state of refraining of taking part on either side."

We ask: Has the public school in the United States been neutral in the matter of religion? If neutrality consists in the refusal to become involved in contests or controversies between others, it is true that the public school has always been neutral in the controversies between the various contending groups of what has been referred to as the "Protestant Establishment." The religious practices recently outlawed by the Supreme Court, namely prayer and Bible reading, were "neutral" in the sense that they did not entangle the school in the controversies between various Protestant groups, since on these matters Protestants were in substantial agreement.

The public school has not always been neutral, however, in the controversy between Protestants and Catholics and Jews or in the contest between people who believe in God and people who do not. The practices of the past meant that the public school took part on the side of the Protestant consensus against those who did not share in it.

The recent ill–fated effort on the part of the Board of Regents of the State of New York to write a prayer for use

[7] *Ibid.*, p. 172.

in that state's public schools was, in fact, an attempt to include in the consensus all God–believing people and to establish neutrality on the broadest possible basis. The prayer in question—"Almighty God, we acknowledge our dependence upon thee, and we beg thy blessings upon us, our parents, our teachers and our country"—was designed to extricate the public school from any controversy between contending religious groups. It was, however, not neutral between those who believed in God and those who did not believe. It was, therefore, held unconstitutional by the Supreme Court in the *Engel vs Vitale* decision.

Neutrality as presently defined prohibits the public school not only from taking sides between the contending religious groups, but also between theists, deists, pantheists, agnostics, and atheists, in short, those who believe in God and those who do not.

But even if we grant that complete neutrality on the part of the public school as ordered by the Supreme Court is the fairest solution to the vexing problem of religion in a pluralistic society where a religious consensus is simply not present, the real question remains: How is this neutrality to be implemented? When I talk about the "illusion of neutrality" I desire to suggest that it is possible to pay lip–service to this non-involvement in religious controversy while implicitly taking sides. The danger is great that an easy and superficial compliance with the Supreme Court decisions might involve the school in the religious controversy as an active participant on the side of atheism and actually pervert the intention of the court's decision. This would happen if neutrality would be interpreted to mean that the phenomenon "religion" and all it involves would be ignored by the public school in order to assure its neutrality.

If religious documents like the Bible, the Koran, or the Bhagavadgita are not studied in the public school when and where their study would contribute to the understand-

ing of a culture—because they are religious documents—
neutrality has become obscurantism and partisanship on
behalf of what Justices Goldberg and Harlan called, "a
brooding and pervasive devotion to the secular and a passive or even active hostility to the religious."

Similarly, if in a study of the European Middle Ages or
the sixteenth century in Germany religious issues are ignored and these periods of history are interpreted with the
help of politics or economics exclusively, without reference
to religious ideas and ideals, the school would in fact become a partisan of an aggressive secularism which mali-
ciously or ignorantly claims that religious issues are of no
significance, and that all cultural development can and
should be explained in exclusively economic or political
terms.

If, as seems to be the case, the student in public school is
allowed to study everything from accounting to zoology—
including driver training—but prohibited from investigating
the great religious traditions of mankind in general and
America in particular, this is not neutrality, but the most
flagrant partisanship against the study of a subject which
has been studied by learned and wise men since the beginning of human history, producing some of the most impressive literary expressions of the human spirit from Moses and
Confucius to Rada Krishna, Martin Buber, Paul Tillich, Karl
Barth, Albert Schweitzer, and Pierre Teilhard de Chardin in
our own time.

To exclude American public school students from this,
their common human heritage, on the grounds of pretended
neutrality, is the crassest secularistic partisanship. If education is to open windows of the mind, not close them, such
an approach must be termed anti–educational obfuscation.

Unbelievable as it seems, this approach has, however,
been advocated as the proper attitude of the public school
for two reasons. One is the allegation that religion is not a

proper subject for study, that it is obsolete and belongs no more in an educational curriculum than, let us say, the study of astrology. The very tone in which this claim has been made reveals the spokesmen as partisans of the religion of atheism. To listen to them would, indeed, make the public school a sectarian institution—promoting an atheistic faith. This identification of the public schools with a minority religion, namely atheism, would be no more justified than their advocacy of the religious consensus. Yet whenever the school acts as if religion did not exist, it allies itself, willingly or not, with this esoteric sectarianism.

The second reason for excluding religion from the educational concern of the public school is far more meritorious. It has been said, and not without reason, that to deal with religion in the public schools of a pluralistic society is difficult and can easily involve the school, the teacher, and the student in conflicts of conscience which should be avoided at all costs. Here the claim is, that while religion is a subject that merits attention, the existential involvement of students and teachers in the phenomenon makes an educationally creative discussion of the subject impossible. As one who has taught religion for more than twenty years and on four continents, I would be the first to admit the difficulties which the existential involvement of the teachers and students in the subject produces. But since when is it the task of the school to deal only with simple and non–controversial matters? In a religiously pluralistic country that has great responsibilities in a religiously pluralistic world, it is of the essence that the pervasive and powerful phenomenon we call "religion" be intelligently and comprehensively understood. Unless all our citizens are sensitized to the issues involved through intelligent teaching and diligent study, we will forever react like the proverbial "bull in the china shop" when confronted with the intricacies of religious tensions in places like Viet Nam or Cyprus, to use only two recent examples. In these complex situations, the tawdry attitude of the village atheist is not really helpful, even if the particular village atheist has a Ph.D. Thus, in spite of the admitted difficulties which the study of religion implies, the cultural importance of the subject makes the involvement of the school unavoidable. It would be best if it were approached openly and unapologetically as a worthy and fascinating part of any educational curriculum. To ignore it or to put it aside as a marginal concern easily subsumed under other courses is prejudicial to the important subject of religion and to sound and comprehensive public education.

But in order to deal fairly with the reality of religion in the educational program of the American public school, certain basic conditions will have to be met.

The distinction between worship and education must be clearly made. The school is an educational institution, not a church. Religion belongs in the public school as a subject for study; worship is the responsibility of the home and the church.

The sensitive and delicate character of the religious commitment should be noted. In dealing with religion in its many forms, the school must show an awareness of the special character of this phenomenon. A purely quantitative approach to the subject will not create but destroy all understanding. As the subject of sex must be handled with tact and good taste, so the subject of religion demands sensitivity and discernment.

The teacher called upon to deal with this subject must have special training. While this seems like a fairly obvious requirement, it is a serious obstacle to the public school's intelligent involvement. We do not have people educated to teach religion in public school. In fact, even on the college level, it is not uncommon that people who teach courses about the Bible as literature have never had a professional course like "Introduction to the Old Testament" or "Introduction to the New Testament." They hardly ever know Hebrew or Greek and are thus quite unprepared to teach the subject by the standards applicable to other subjects. But because of the common assumption that everybody is an expert in religion, be he politician, movie star, or heavyweight boxing champion, many erroneously believe that one can teach religion without having studied it. While this attitude is unfortunate in Sunday School, it would be disastrous in public school. What is true in physics and French is true in religion as well: before we teach we have to learn.

The study of religion, while important, should be elective in public school. This is to avoid conflicts of conscience for those who would find a non–devotional approach to the subject offensive. While many of us might regret their unwillingness to study this fascinating subject, the right to avoid such courses should be guaranteed.

We began our presentation by an examination of the concept of neutrality, which has characterized the Supreme Court approach to religion on the part of the public school. We claimed that given our situation in America, neutrality is probably the fairest and most constructive approach to religion open to the public school.

Yet we also observed, as the court had indicated, that neutrality can become an illusion. It can become a device to make the public school the aggressive instrument of the religion of secularism. This may happen surreptitiously if the problems implicit in the concept of neutrality are not openly faced.

The remedy open to the public school is to teach about the phenomenon of religion frankly and sensitively. If this were done by competent and perceptive people, neutrality would not be an illusion and the school would contribute substantially to the education of young Americans for intelligent citizenship in a religiously pluralistic world. Religion is here to stay. In its many different expressions, it has been one of the great forces which have shaped man and his destiny. Some of us might say that man is most characteristically human in his religion. Thus we should try to understand our own religion and that of our neighbor—be he next door or across the Pacific Ocean. In this effort to understand, the public school can play an important part if it has the courage to be a truly educational institution.

VI

THE
UNIVERSITY'S ETHICAL
CRISIS

Theologians seem to have the reputation of being unnecessarily verbose and obscure. In an effort to counteract this prevalent impression, let me begin by limiting and defining the subject, then stating three brief theses and defending them as clearly as I am able.

This presentation will not deal with the university outside of the United States. The literature would indicate that there is such a phenomenon as a crisis in the university in Europe. Ernst Anrich's book *Die Idee der Universität und die Reform der deutschen Universitäten*,[1] e.g., is a perceptive diagnosis and an eloquent call to reform, but this is beyond the purview of this discussion. The crisis in British or Asian universities will not be mentioned either. University shall mean American university.

Furthermore, the term "university" is going to be used in the peculiarly ambiguous and imprecise manner typical for American usage. Neal, in the 1747 edition of his *History of New England*, set a pattern of linguistic imprecision so far as terminology dealing with academic institutions is concerned that has been with us ever since. He described Harvard in the following words:

> There are several fine streets and good houses in it, besides a flourishing academy consisting of two spacious colleges built of brick, called by the name of Harvard College and

[1] Wissenschaftliche Buchgesellschaft, Darmstadt, 1960.

Stoughton Hall, which are under the government of one
president, five fellows, and a treasurer [who] are the imme-
diate governors of the *college*. The learned and ingenious
Mr. John Leverett is now President of this *seminary* . . .
the *academy* is this year in a very flourishing condition . . .
I have given a particular account of the foundation of this
university.[2]

Neal managed to use the terms "college," "academy," "seminary," and "university" almost interchangeably, and this has
been the fate of those words ever since. This is neither the
place nor the time to produce a precision of language which
would at best be arbitrary, and at worst add further confusion.

Furthermore, I accept David Riesman's image of American academia as a "snake-like" procession with institutions
at the head moving in one direction and institutions in the
middle and in the tail of the snake apparently going in
different directions. He speaks of shifts among the avant-
garde institutions concerned with "general education," "theology," "values"; the democratization of academic pioneer-
ing, in the middle; and the torpor in the tail of the
procession.[3]

Yet it is my claim that all of these varying institutions are
actually related so that one can speak of the university and
include the entire "snake." In fact, some of the movements
and countermovements in this body are more interdependent than might at first appear.

This serpentine structure of the American academic community has certain obvious consequences when evaluating
academic phenomena. It means, for example, that all state-
ments made by the participants in this snake-like procession
must be seen in the context of the place in the body of this

[2] As quoted in David Riesman, *Constraint and Variety in American
Education* (New York: Doubleday Anchor Books, 1958), p. 62.
[3] *Ibid.*, pp. 35 ff.

snake where they find themselves. Thus, it is eminently proper to speak of Plato and Aristotle to the freshmen students raised on comic books and second–rate high school texts, and it may be equally in order to speak of the significance of comic strips like Peanuts and Pogo to freshmen students who have read Eliot and Faulkner, Salinger and Updike in their preparatory schools.

Within the context of the place of the procession where they find themselves, these approaches—though apparently contradictory—may be essentially consistent. It is one thing to speak of football as the American form of the ballet at a school where football is an activity rated just behind fencing and just ahead of badminton. It is another thing altogether to use this alleged Santayana quotation about football at a school where the football season is the highpoint of the academic year.

In short, a remark is appropriate if it broadens the vision of the student, inappropriate if it further restricts it; whether it does one or the other will depend to a considerable degree on the place in the procession where one happens to be. But the university in this discussion is the entire snake–like procession in whatever direction the particular segment of the body of the snake on which we are located may happen to move.

Finally, ethical crisis simply means here uncertainty and conflict in the area of values, of right and wrong, of good and bad.

Now it is my first obvious, and admittedly platitudinous, thesis that ethical conflicts are as old as man and have always been part of the life of the university. In the most obvious sense these conflicts are less severe in America today than they have been in the past.

Students misbehaved in the judgment of their parents and teachers at Bologna and Salerno, at Oxford and Cambridge, at Wittenberg and Geneva. If anything, they study harder and play less than they used to do. If I speak of ethical crisis, I do not mean "sex on the campus."

Even professors are not worse than they used to be They have squabbled and engaged in unsavory academic politics since there has been a university. If anything, we have become more polite and perhaps more "ethical." It is not professorial behavior that makes us speak of an ethical crisis. Not even the administration should be made the scapegoat. While there are certainly far more administrators today than in the ancient universities—or even when I began my work as a teacher a number of years ago—their presence is, faculty comment to the contrary notwithstanding, not an unmitigated evil. They relieve the teachers of the task of soliciting students, which seems to have taken up a good deal of time in the "good old days"; they assure regular paychecks for the faculty, being spectacularly more successful in collecting fees from students, gifts from alumni and others, and subsidies from governments than the professors were when they tried to do it themselves. They have their ethical problems, but they are hardly the cause of the crisis.

If we are, indeed, unhappy with the ethical level of academic politics, it is probably because in view of our academic pretensions we expect too much. Many of us know that politics in the church is so singularly depressing because of the religious pretensions used to camoflage the struggle for power in this divine–human society. The tendency to use the wings of the Holy Spirit to cover the wound in the back of the opponent makes the political stab in the back even more revolting.

Similarly in the university, the use of academic freedom, scientific objectivity, and the untrammeled search for truth to cover grabs for power, departmental homogeneity, and bootlicking tends to depress all of us. These are certainly important ethical issues, but there is no evidence that in this respect the situation today is worse than it used to be. Indeed, if my secondary sources have not deceived me, there is a good deal of evidence that so far as academic freedom and fair treatment of faculty is concerned, the situation in America has improved spectacularly in the last fifty years.

There was a time when the University of Chicago, then contemptuously called the "Gas Trust University," could and did fire a teacher for delivering a speech against the railroad companies while the Pullman strike was going on. The professor, Edward W. Bemis, had said, "If the railroads expect their men to be law–abiding, they must set the example. Let their open violation of the interstate commerce law and the relations to corrupt legislatures and assessors testify as to their part in this regard. . . . Let there be some equality in the treatment of these things."[4] As a result of this speech and the speaker's effort to deal with a major ethical issue of the time, he received the following letter from the famous William Rainey Harper, then President of the University of Chicago. It speaks for itself: "Your speech," he wrote, "has caused me a great deal of annoyance. It is hardly safe for me to venture into any of the Chicago clubs. I am pounced upon from all sides. I propose that during the remainder of your connection with the University you exercise very great care in public utterance about questions that are agitating the minds of the people."[5] At the end of the academic year, Bemis' appointment was not renewed.

The remark of a Northwestern University trustee at the turn of the century was by no means atypical: "As to what should be taught in political and social science, they [the professors] should promptly and gracefully submit to the determination of the trustees when the latter find it neces-

[4] As quoted in Walter P. Metzger, *Academic Freedom in the Age of the University* (New York: Columbia University Press, 1961), p. 153.
[5] *Ibid.*, p. 154.

sary to act. . . . If the trustees err it is for the patrons and proprietors not for the employees, to change either the policy or the personnel of the board."[6]

Yet in state–controlled universities, the situation was not significantly different. At Kansas State Agricultural College, for example, a political change in the state government resulted in the dismissal of the President and the appointment of Populists to the chairs in the social sciences. Three years later, when the Republicans returned to power, the policy was again reversed, and President and the Populist social scientists dismissed and replaced with reliable Republicans.[7]

It is depressing to contemplate that as recently as World War I, the A.A.U.P. endorsed principles for the dismissal of professors which, except for the first, were giving free rein to the witch-hunters. It gave (in a statement composed by A. A. Lovejoy, Edward Capps, and A. A. Young) four reasons for legitimately dismissing professors:

1. Conviction of disobedience to any statute or lawful executive order relating to the war.

2. Propaganda designed, or unmistakably tending, to cause others to resist or evade the compulsory service law or the regulation of the military authorities.

3. Action designated to dissuade others from rendering voluntary assistance to the efforts of the government.

4. In the case of professors of Teutonic extraction and sympathy, violating the obligation to refrain from public discussion of the war, and in their private intercourse with neighbors, colleagues, and students, to avoid all hostile or offensive expressions concerning the United States or its government.[8]

[6] *Ibid.*, p. 185.
[7] *Ibid.*, pp. 150 f.
[8] *Ibid.*, p. 230.

Compared with this flagrant surrender of academic freedom by its alleged guardians, such freedom seems today on
far firmer foundation. Most of us, I am sure, feel free to
speak on any issue within our professional competence
without fear of recrimination. I personally have taught in a
small denominational college, a theological seminary, and
a state university, and academic freedom was simply taken
for granted in all these institutions.

In fact, the mantle of academic freedom has tended to
cover for us many remarks quite removed from our academic competence. Under this mantle, professors of classics
have acted as political oracles, and professors of sociology
have used it to give authority to their more or less informed
theological observations before open–mouthed freshmen
who could not easily tell where sociologically competent
information ended and the remarks of the village atheist
began. If anything, the *obiter dicta* of the professors have
achieved a halo, which, in fact, they hardly deserve.

On the basis of this perhaps too rosy picture of the present situation, can we indeed speak of an ethical crisis in the
university? My answer is, and this is my second thesis, an
unqualified "yes." The ethical crisis that engulfs us is of a
different kind than student morality, professorial politics,
administrative pretense, or even academic freedom. We are
experiencing a crisis of Truth, with a capital T. Riesman has
described the present situation as follows: "American higher
education seems to be directionless at the head of the procession as far as major innovations are concerned, in rapid,
if sometimes contradictory motion in the middle and lack-
ing much, if any aliveness at the end."[9] I propose that the
reason for this apparent aimlessness at the head of the procession, among the most learned, the most sophisticated, is
ethical. It is the result of the dawning realization that edu-

[9] Riesman, *op. cit.*, p. 64.

cation, or even science, does not save, that it cannot supply the ultimate answers, if indeed, such answers exist.

This skepticism in regard to the possibilities of science and education is something new in America. Higher education in this country was started by people who were hopeful that Christian scholarship and Christian education could eventually supply the answers to men's problems. While the fathers might disagree on the version of Christianity which would be the best road to these answers, the existence of teachable truth that shall make men free was a common possession of Baptists and Roman Catholics, Lutherans, and Calvinists.

The rise of the secular university did not really change this confidence in a liberating truth, which had been or could be discovered, now, of course, without help of revelation and theology by means of the scientific method and painstaking research. There was, however, very little difference in the basic mind-set of those who believed in salvation by Christian education and those who believed in salvation by scientific education. The inscription "The truth shall make you free" could be left on the library building even after the last clergyman had been replaced by a businessman or politician on the governing board. The job was going to be done; it was merely a different Truth which was going to do it.

It was symptomatic that even after World War II, a distinguished, if elderly, social scientist could write a book *Can Science Save?* and answer the unmistakable revivalistic question with a thundering "Yes." There is really very little difference between the preacher in the fundamentalist church who informs his congregation Sunday after Sunday how he has found Jesus, and the preacher in the liberal church around the corner who informs his congregation Sunday after Sunday how he has lost him. It is not too surprising that a good many members of the latter congregation were raised in the former. They are used to this subjective, unhistorical, and moralistic type of approach and could not do without it.

Similarly, the switch from salvation by acceptance of theological propositions to salvation by acceptance of psychoanalytic, economic, or semantic propositions was not really as radical as it appeared. There still was Truth that could make men free, and the universities could communicate it. As once there had been Christian answers to all questions, we now had psychoanalytical, biochemical, economic—in short, "scientific" answers to all questions, or at least the method to obtain them.

It is my conviction that the current ethical crisis in the university is caused by the fact that many, if not most, of us no longer believe this. We no longer believe in any Truth, with a capital T, which can be attained by man either by means of theology or the more recent arrivals in the field of science.

There are, indeed, many answers which we can find, but each answer raises new and subtle questions. We thus read with a certain nostalgia the so-called Wisconsin *Magna Charta*: "Whatever may be the limitations which trammel inquiry elsewhere, we believe the great State University of Wisconsin should ever encourage that continual and fearless sifting and winnowing by which alone the truth can be found."[10]

The reason for our sadness is that we no longer believe in *the* Truth at the end of the rainbow of scientific inquiry, and this is the basis for the university's ethical crisis. Right and wrong, good and bad, once so clearly discernible to all professors, are thus no longer.

If you have generally agreed with me so far, you may not be surprised that my third thesis is that as a theologian

[10] Metzger, *op. cit.*, p. 153.

of the Christian church, I welcome this development and would like you to welcome it with me. The university, both in the form of the Christian college and the secular university was *überfordert*, as the Germans would say—asked to do something it could not possibly accomplish—when it was asked to save man or make him free. It could not possibly meet this demand. Thus, our present crisis, far from being a disaster, is a sign of maturity. By limiting our inquiries to the truths that can be discovered by the application of man's intellect and imagination, we are freed to do our task with humility and zeal. We are free from the illegitimate question of whether anybody is going to be saved by our scholarly effort.

The university deals with the penultimate; it should not (using Bonhoeffer's phrase) be asked to give ultimate answers to penultimate questions. Or, to use another formulation, the university belongs to the realm of law; it should not be asked to produce a gospel.

This is as important for the theologian as it is for the sociologist or nuclear physicist. The theologian cannot produce saving faith; he can study it, explain it, clarify it for the community that shares this faith, as well as for those who do not share it. This is his legitimate function, and because such faith in its many expressions is an important and central aspect of man's humility, such investigation and clarification is a legitimate task of every serious university.

But the theologian cannot produce faith and never could. The notion that any human being can ultimately save any other is an expression of intellectual *hubris*. Salvation is by grace alone. No college can domesticate the Holy Spirit so that his activity can be dispensed by the faculty as part of the curriculum. Colleges that pretend to do this travel under false colors.

But if theological science cannot offer salvation, neither can the social sciences, the humanities, or the natural sciences. If the theological pretensions were *hubris,* so are the salvatory pretensions of the others. Nobody in the university has the Truth which can make man free at his disposal. Nietzsche's attack against pietist Christians holds equally true for the fraudulent claims of our more recent purveyors of scientific salvation: "More like saved ones they would have to look before I believe in their savior."

Salvation is not man's to give. Truth with a capital T is not ours to dispense. Far from deploring the ethical crisis in the university resulting from this realization, let us welcome it, learn to live with it, and see what it may mean to us as Christians in the university.

For the first time, the university can be truly secular, not secularistic, but secular, pursuing the truths men can discover by the use of their vision and their reason. While this pursuit of penultimate answers to penultimate questions will not save us or make us free, it may contribute to greater knowledge, a fuller life, and, God willing, the earthly welfare of man. Though this may not be all we desire, these limited objectives are worthy goals for us to pursue.

While we Christians believe that the earth is the Lord's and the fullness thereof—including the university and all its legitimate concerns—we do not believe that this faith makes us better scholars or teachers than our colleagues who do not share it. If they too are satisfied to attain limited objectives and do not let the obsession with *the* Truth that man cannot achieve but must receive obscure their search for those truths men can discover with the tools available to them, i.e., imagination and reason, they will contribute no less than we to this human effort.

What we consider to be the ultimate truth is not at our disposal or even within our reach. It is God's gift obtained by grace alone. "To accept our acceptance in spite of the fact that we are not acceptable" (Tillich) will be given to us in God's good time. The truth that makes man free comes to us *in vocatione*, that is, while doing our job, not *per vocationem*, that is, as a result of doing our job particularly well. It will be given to those who are called to work in the university *while* they do their work humbly and faithfully, not *because* they do it in a particularly "religious" or "scientific" manner.

Yet in the obvious and profound ethical crisis in the university caused by the disappearance of the integrating principle which truth with a capital T, however dubiously, did supply, Christians have a witness, a message to bear.

From the perspective of our faith in the person who to us is the Way, the Truth, and the Life, we must say with him to ourselves and to our colleagues, "You who labor in the university, remember as the Sabbath was made for man and not man for the Sabbath, so the university was made for man and not man for the university." The university is not an end in itself; scholarship, research, teaching, all have to be seen in the light of our obligation to man, to the neighbor, to each other. We do not serve God in his aseity, as he is in himself, but rather as he has made himself known to us. He confronts us in the neighbor, especially the neighbor in need. In this world, to serve God means to serve man. And this is as true in the university as everywhere else.

In this concern for man, the service of man even in our life as members of the academic community, we will probably be joined by all sorts of unexpected allies: adherents of non–Christian religions, agnostics, professed atheists. For reasons good and sufficient to them they will work with us on behalf of man. We should thank God for every one of them and bear our witness to the truth that was given us gladly—in faith, hope, and love; but the greatest of these is love.

VII

SOME IMPLICATIONS
OF THE AXIOMS OF CLASSICAL
PROTESTANTISM FOR THE PHILOSOPHY
OF EDUCATION

The basic purpose of this essay is very simple: to convey some information concerning contemporary Protestant theology as seen by an insider. It is addressed to the common concerns of men and women whose business it is to articulate philosophy of education and those whose business it is to interpret Protestant theology.

I speak from within the context of what is often called "Classical protestantism," essentially the theological position formulated by the reformers of the sixteenth century. It is my claim that a consensus which one can call classical Protestantism does in fact exist, and that the faith of this particular Christian tradition may be defined in the following three axioms: *Sola Gratia*, the insistence upon grace and the sovereignty of God; *Sola Fide*, the insistence upon justification by faith; and *Sola Scriptura*, the insistence upon Scripture as the Rule of Faith. Certainly there are other aspects of this tradition, but it is in these three axioms that the proclamation of classical Protestantism has been summarized, and therefore we shall survey them briefly.

GRACE AND THE SOVEREIGNTY OF GOD

In his so–called Small Catechism, which eventually became one of the confessional documents of the church of the Augsburg Confession, Martin Luther says in the explanation of the third article of the Apostles' Creed:

> I believe that I cannot by my own reason or strength believe in Jesus Christ my Lord, or come to Him; but the Holy Ghost has called me through the Gospel, enlightened me by His gifts, and sanctified and preserved me in the true faith; in the like manner as he calls, gathers, enlightens, and sanctifies the whole Christian Church on earth, and preserves it in union with Jesus Christ in the true faith.

The insistence that man cannot by his own reason or strength save himself is the assertion that God alone can establish the God–man relationship. Man has no power of his own to save himself. This is the classical emphasis on "by grace alone."

This axiomatic assertion has all sorts of obvious consequences. It implies that it is impossible for men to produce Christians by education; God's adoption of man is always a miracle. In the words of one of the greatest Protestant theologians of our time:

> What occurs here between God and man is no less great a miracle than that of Christmas or of Easter. With the confessing of Christ's birth the Holy Spirit also is mentioned, and it is not in vain: "Conceived of the Holy Ghost." The same Holy Spirit repeats this miracle of the virgin birth whenever someone comes to believe, to see the whole of his life "in Jesus Christ," to enter the Church, to receive remission of sins and hope of the everlasting future.[1]

Implied in this understanding of the nature of the relationship between God and man is the rejection of all those efforts to reach God which are commonly associated with religion.

"By grace alone" means that all religious legalism must be ruled out. Any effort to establish a claim upon God by

[1] Karl Barth, *The Faith of the Church* (New York: Meridian Books, 1958), p. 127.

conforming to a certain behavior pattern represents a subversion of the sovereign grace of God. While it is true that empirical Protestantism has frequently been quite enthusiastic in its adoption of legalism, it must be added that whenever this was the case it implied the denial of a basic axiom of the Protestant faith. There is no way in which man can establish a claim upon God; salvation is always God's free and unmerited gift.

"By grace alone" means also that classical Protestantism must reject rationalism in all its forms. Neither by obedience to law, nor by the exercise of one's reason can God be attained. It is here that we find the reason for the de-emphasis of all so-called proofs for the existence of God. Similarly, the suspicion that theological systems, be they ever so correct, have no power to save is based upon the axiom "by grace alone." To insist that the existence of God is demonstrable by reason—as some Christians do—is not part of the Protestant proclamation. Since reason, like all other human faculties, is distorted by sin, it cannot be trusted to bring man to a certain knowledge of God. Classical Protestantism has been generally skeptical of all efforts to entrust unaided human reason with the task of establishing any relationship between man and God.

"By grace alone" means also that classical Protestantism rejects the mystical efforts, the ladder to paradise, the exercises of the imagination, which have in the view of many religious people procured them access to God. There is no method, no practice, no human effort which enables man to reach God. Indeed, all these human efforts may lead to pride and thus actually increase and perpetuate the separation of God and man and obstruct God's way to man. Luther commented on the mystical prophets of his time, such as Thomas Muenzer, that they sounded "as if they had swallowed the Holy Spirit, feathers and all," and he distrusted them profoundly.

But what does this insistence upon "by grace alone" mean for the conversation of theologians and educators? It appears that the Protestant community, in principle, not only cannot demand that the educational process be used to manufacture faith, but would deny that it could produce true faith even if this were its stated objective. The understanding of the relationship between God and man which classical Protestantism proclaims denies that there is a method, a technique, which can capture the work of the Holy Spirit. However, the acceptance of this axiom does not free the school, in the view of Protestants, from the task of helping students to come to a full understanding of their culture and of themselves. The school can indeed convey information and religion can be the object of study. In fact, an adequate education should treat religion in general and the Hebrew–Christian tradition in particular in a manner commensurate with its importance in our culture. While the school or university cannot and should not attempt to produce faith, it can and should convey accurate and relevant information. It appears that in the whole area of religion it is failing to do so. The result is a skewed education. For the abysmal ignorance of the facts of the Hebrew–Christian tradition which characterize the modern American is not only a handicap for him as a churchman but is also a threat to him as a civilized human being. This ignorance, obviously the result of the inability of our educational system to handle this touchy subject, admittedly affects the teaching in many other areas of the curriculum and threatens to become a public scandal. It is at this point that an open and frank conversation between theologians and educators might help to remedy the deplorable present situation.

JUSTIFICATION BY FAITH

The response to God's grace is faith. Formally, as Tillich puts it, faith is "a total and centered act of the personal self, the act of unconditional, infinite, and ultimate concern."[2] Materially, the Christian faith is the complete trust in Jesus Christ as the revelation of God and the key to the meaning of life. Calvin wrote:

> We shall have a complete definition of faith, if we say, that it is a steady and certain knowledge of the divine benevolence towards us, which being founded on the truth of the gratuitous promise in Christ, is both revealed to our minds, and confirmed to our hearts by the Holy Spirit.[3]

Faith can be distorted by emphasizing one element of it to the exclusion of all others. Paul Tillich speaks of three such distortions of the meaning of faith.

One he calls the intellectualistic distortion of the meaning of faith. This is to interpret faith by considering it "an act of knowledge having a low degree of evidence." But faith does not affirm or deny knowledge of our world. As Whitehead pointed out, most so–called conflicts between science and religion are the result of dubious approaches.[4] Either the representatives of religion claim the sanction of religion for knowledge of our world which is a matter of scientific inquiry, or, and this is actually more common in our time, representatives of science are consciously or unconsciously hiding their faith, in the sense of ultimate concern, behind an allegedly pure scientific method.

The implications for the conversation between theologians and educators are obvious. We need the academic equivalent of a pure food and drug law. This does not mean that religious people are not entitled to their scientific idiosyncrasies. However, they should be seen as such and not as necessary concomitants of faith. Similarly, any scientist is

[2] Paul Tillich, *Dynamics of Faith* (New York: Harper & Row, 1958), p. 8.

[3] John Calvin, *Institutes of the Christian Religion*, John Allen, trans., Vol. I (Philadelphia: Presbyterian Board of Education, 1936), p. 604.

[4] *Cf.* Alfred N. Whitehead, *Science and the Modern World* (New York: Mentor Books, 1948), p. 180 ff.

entitled to his own expression of ultimate concern, but it would contribute a great deal to education if this concern were not camouflaged behind the smoke-screen of a so-called scientific method.

A second possible distortion of faith Tillich calls the voluntaristic distortion of the meaning of faith. This is the attempt to use faith as a tool, as the will to believe. Here one makes up through the exertion of the will what one lacks in evidence. Faith is distorted if it is not the result of God's sovereign grace, but rather the result of man's will to believe. Faith, if genuine, always comes before obedience. The faith which is merely the result of the will to believe is not faith at all. As Tillich puts it, "Finite man cannot produce infinite concern. Our oscillating will cannot produce the certainty which belongs to faith."[5]

In the discussion between theology and education this means that the lack or absence of faith cannot and should not be held against anybody. Even if a religious community had the power to demand faith it would not have the right to do so. Forced religious commitment is an offense against the nature of faith. But this is true of all attempts to enforce infinite concern. A forced commitment to democracy or man or the American Way of Life as an ultimate concern is as undesirable as the forced commitment to Jesus Christ as Lord and Savior. An understanding of the nature of faith as ultimate concern makes the attempts to produce a common faith highly dubious. And quite obviously the empirical church is neither the only nor the most subtle offender against the principle.

Tillich calls the third distortion of the meaning of faith the emotional distortion. Since Schleiermacher, it has been customary among friends and foes of religion to relegate faith to the realm of feeling. Religious people saw in this a safe refuge from the encroachments by natural and social

5 Tillich, *op. cit.*, p. 38.

science. Those who abhorred religion felt that the ghetto of subjective feeling was sufficiently far from man's important activities to make religion harmless. The result of this placement of faith was that it was understood as an essentially arbitrary subjective taste, marginal and irrational as one's taste in food or games. Thus it could be ignored; *de gustibus non est disputandum.* As the private affair of some individuals, it was irrelevant to the entire process of culture. This isolation of faith falsified the religion of those who accepted it. Faith as subjective taste does have little in common with the faith of classical Protestantism. As we have shown, if it is merely taste it isn't faith at all. For those who had hoped that by this placement of faith they might be permanently rid of ultimate concern, it developed that this effort at eliminating it was quite futile. Ultimate concern, much less clearly labeled, turned up everywhere playing havoc with science and culture. The age of the "gods that failed" had dawned.

Here, too, certain implications for education seem evident. Faith cannot be merely subjective emotion. "Faith as the state of ultimate concern claims the whole man and cannot be restricted to the subjectivity of mere feeling."[6] This means that the isolation of faith from culture, whether desired by the religious or by the irreligious, is impossible. Ultimate concern has to be faced. In a pluralistic society it should be faced in accordance with the realities of this society. But to ignore faith is obscurantist and dangerous. It has become almost ridiculous how the fact of faith is being ignored or obscured by many allegedly enlightened people. One is tempted to draw the parallel to the nineteenth century, when the fact of sex was equally ignored. It seems now that this effort of the nineteenth century did not succeed in abolishing sex. It seems unlikely that the efforts of the twentieth century will succeed in abolishing faith. As a

[6] Tillich, *op. cit.*, p. 39.

fact of life, faith ought to be made the subject of study, whatever one's own faith. The time is ripe for our universities to lead the way in a realistic and sympathetic study of one of the basic if not the ultimate concerns of man.

SCRIPTURE AS THE RULE OF FAITH

Holy Scripture containeth all things necessary to salvation: so whatsoever is not read therein, nor may be proved thereby is not to be required of any man, that it should be believed as article of faith, or be thought requisite or necessary to salvation. (Anglican Articles of Religion)

It is a common emphasis of classical Protestantism that Scripture is the norm of faith. This means that God's deeds for man as recorded in the Old and New Testaments show forth the gracious and redemptive activity of God. The history of Israel and the early church is the record of God's revelatory action, the story of his redemptive purpose. The proclamation of the church is the proclamation of what God has done, is doing, and will do.

This assertion must be guarded against the tendency to make the Bible into a collection of theological propositions from which a true philosophy of life can be logically deduced. Indeed, this unhistorical view of scripture as a volume of infallible quotations has occasionally overcome Protestantism. The essentially antihistorical method of allegorization did much to obscure the Bible as the record of *Heilsgeschichte*. Both Luther and Calvin consciously opposed allegorization—though occasionally they fell unconsciously prey to it.

In our time, fundamentalism with its docetic view of Scripture—denying it its humanity—has done much to make the very Scripture it tried to exalt appear irrelevant and obscure. Scripture as the proclamation of God's action resists all efforts to force the church's proclamation into the procrustean bed of any philosophy. Each generation has to find its own language to proclaim God's deeds in a manner adequate to the needs of its time. To this end it must be free to adapt whatever philosophy or language will help to communicate God's deeds best. It must, to borrow Luther's phrase, *den Leuten aufs Maul schauen,* "pick up the idiom of the people" to whom the deeds of God are to be made known.

Protestant theology cannot be permanently Aristotelian or existentialist, idealist or empiricist, yet theologians will try to learn from all of these interpretations if they are the speech of the time. This is the clue to the effort of Bultmann and the demythologizers in Europe. Here the philosophy of Heidegger is used as a means for the communication of the *kerygma.* Bultmann is quite frank about this. "Our task," he says, "is to produce an existentialist interpretation of the dualistic mythology of the New Testament."[7] And in another place, "Heidegger's existentialist analysis of the ontological structure of being would seem to be no more than a secularized, philosophical version of the New Testament view of human life."[8] The accuracy of this observation is debatable, yet the interest of Bultmann is quite clear. He is looking for language which will enable the church to proclaim the biblical *kerygma* in the twentieth century. His concern is essentially evangelical.

And the same is true for those British philosophers and theologians like Ian Ramsey, Antony Flew, Alasdair MacIntyre, and many others who try to utilize logical empiricism for the proclamation of this *kerygma.* Ramsey, for example, says:

> We have seen how important logical empiricism can be for theological analysis, and in particular how it can help us to clarify Christian controversies by elucidating the logical

[7] Hans Werner Bartsch, ed., *Kerygma and Myth,* Reginald Fuller, trans. (London: S.P.C.K., 1957), p. 16.
[8] *Ibid.,* p. 24.

placings of traditional Christian phrases. But make no mistake, I do not claim that here is something altogether new.
We might well admit that in principle we are only doing
what, for example, St. Thomas Aquinas was doing, though
we are not thereby committed (for better or worse) to his
ontology and system. . . . If the reader thinks that logical
empiricism will have a tendency to make theology "verbal"
he is right if he means by this that it would invent no
"entities" beyond necessity. But at the same time I would
emphasize that in the end the one "factual" reference it
preserves is the one which alone matters, the one that is
given in worship. God and his worship; logical empiricism,
put to the service of theology, starts and ends there.[9]

Again, one might very well disagree with the method here
utilized, but the concern is obviously not the elaboration or
defense of a philosophy in competition with other philos-
ophies but the service of God. Philosophy is so clearly
ancillary to the kerygmatic task in Protestantism that any
particular philosophical system can be abandoned without
endangering the biblical norm. Certainly in Paul Tillich's
Systematic Theology, philosophy plays a most important
part. Here Jacob Boehme, Goethe, Schelling, Nietzsche, the
depth–psychologists, and many others are constantly used.
Indeed, Tillich states that "the situation to which theology
must respond is the totality of man's creative self–interpretation in a special period."[10]
Yet according to him also:

Theology, as a function of the Christian church, must serve
the needs of the church. A theological system is supposed
to satisfy two basic needs: the statement of the truth of the
Christian message and the interpretation of this truth for
every new generation.[11]

[9] Ian T. Ramsey, *Religious Language* (London: SCM Press, 1957), p.
185.
[10] Paul Tillich, *Systematic Theology*, Vol. 1 (Chicago: University of
Chicago Press, 1951), p. 4.
[11] *Ibid.*, p. 3.

Obviously, Protestant theology utilizes philosophy, but the domination of Protestant thought by God's deeds recorded in Scripture makes the type of philosophical elaboration chosen for the Christian proclamation optional. Dominated by the eventful record of Scripture, philosophical reflection becomes secondary. Averse to allegory, Protestantism is shaped by the Bible as the history of God's people.

Are there any implications for the discussion between theologians and educators in this attitude? It would appear that this approach should make for a great openness toward the varieties of educational philosophy. There cannot be any particular educational philosophy which Protestantism could adopt for all time. Rather, since only Scripture is the definitive norm, any historical investigation, logical clarification or philosophical construction will be studied with great interest for the possibilities it offers for the proclamation and elucidation of the *kerygma*—God's deed for man. Protestant theology has always been, is now, and should always remain an open system. This is shown even in so orthodox a theologian as Karl Barth. He says:

> Bible exegesis should be left open on all sides, not, as this demand was put by Liberalism, for the sake of free thinking, but for the sake of a free Bible. Self–defense against possible violence to the text must be left here as everywhere to the text itself, which in practice has so far always succeeded, as a merely spiritual–oral tradition simply cannot, in asserting its own life against encroachments by individuals or whole areas and schools in the church, and in victoriously achieving it in ever-fresh applications, and so in creating recognition of itself as the norm.[12]

And a little later he continues, "The Bible makes itself to be the canon. It is the canon because it has imposed itself as such upon the Church and invariably does so."[13]

[12] Karl Barth, "The Doctrine of the Word of God," *Church Dogmatics*, G. T. Thomson, trans., Vol. I/1 (Edinburgh: T. & T. Clark, 1936), p. 119.
[13] *Ibid.*, p. 120.

Scripture, as the rule of faith, results in the openness of Protestantism to change and revision. If this principle is taken seriously, it rules out the adoption of any other definitive authority, be it of an ideological or administrative nature. The biblical norm, if understood as disclosing normative events, allows for a great deal of elasticity in the Christian's relation to the world, as has been demonstrated all through the history of the Protestant movement.

But Scripture, as the record of what God has done, is doing, and will do, must also be guarded against a tendency to interpret it as just one of many documents which describe the evolution of man's religion from primitive and tribal polytheism to modern and individualistic ethical monotheism. This understanding of Scripture as essentially the document of man's gradual progress, though suggested at times by certain Protestant theologians, is ruled out by its use as the rule of faith in classical Protestantism.

This means the rejection of the automatic and gradual moral evolution of man as untrue to the nature of the biblical witness and realistic in its analysis of the human situation. The notion that history is redemptive cannot be accepted if the record of God's dealing with man as it confronts us in the Old and New Testament is taken seriously. Sin, the alienation of man from God, is so profound and so pervasive that there is no area of personal or collective existence which is not affected by it. This is essentially what the much–maligned doctrine of total depravity asserts. Man does not become better by merely becoming older; this is as true of the entire race as it is true of each individual. We change sins but we do not cease being sinners. It is just in the instant when we believe that we have overcome evil that evil must subtly overcome us.

Classical Protestantism asserts that any interpretation of life which does not take seriously the depth of our estrangement from God, which is the root of our estrangement from the neighbor and from ourselves, is bound to lead to irrelevance or despair. The interpretation of the human situation will be irrelevant whenever it attempts to evade the profundity of the human predicament by suggesting the simple and superficial remedies of legalism. That for many people in contemporary America the Christian answer in particular is identified with such legalism is ironical and depressing. It seems evident that religious people have contributed greatly to the misunderstanding of the nature of the Christian message by identifying their faith with such superficial remedies.

But even a more profound understanding of the human situation, which may avoid the danger of irrelevancy to which legalism always tends, will lead to the other false alternative, namely, despair. When the human predicament is undestood in all its seriousness, when superficial legalism is avoided, then the failure of the individual's and the group's efforts to accomplish their goals leads not infrequently to hopelessness. When it is thought that good will, love, and justice are simple human possibilities and that man is able through his own effort to overcome the guilt, the strife, and the meaninglessness that threaten his life, his failure to achieve his goals may very well result in despair. That such despair, in spite of all surface optimism, is an undercurrent in our society could be shown easily from a look at the barometers of our culture: literature, poetry, and drama. Here the mood is indeed quite somber and Eugene O'Neill's suggestion in *The Iceman Cometh,* that we had better get drunk and stay drunk if we know what is good for us, is symptomatic for an entire generation of perceptive analysis of the mood of twentieth-century man.

The Christian community would insist that such despair is not a possible alternative for those who believe that God's will toward man is revealed in his dealings with his people as recorded in the Old and New Testament. The Bible as the rule of faith excludes a shallow optimism with its confidence in automatic progress and redemptive history. At the same time, it excludes the "despair of God's mercy" expressed in the morbid pessimism which reduces man and history to a "tale told by an idiot full of sound and fury signifying nothing." Classical Protestantism rejects such optimism because it trusts too much in man and it rejects such pessimism because it trusts too little in God.

But what implications can all this possibly have for the conversation between theologians and educators? It appears that if the moods of optimism and pessimism as here described are not entirely unknown in educational circles, it should be suspected that their sources may very well not be the scientific study of education but rather a more or less secularized religious mood which subconsciously determines our thinking. Salvation by education is a dubious dogma, and it does not really become more respectable if its prophets claim to be *bona fide* atheists. Again we need more clear and honest labelling when we speak as scientists and when we speak on the basis of our ultimate concern. Much so-called "scientific" opposition to religion is really the zeal of one religion against another. It is, of course, quite possible to operate with different faith–axioms from those of classical Protestantism. However, it is necessary to be aware of one's faith–axioms and not to hide them behind a smokescreen labelled "science" or "education" or "democracy." To identify one's faith–axioms will not necessarily bring agreement with those who operate with different axioms, but it will make the discussion more honest.

In this presentation, the attempt has been made to describe some of the basic faith–axioms of classical Protestantism and to indicate some possible implications which they might have for discussion between theologians and educators. Of course, these axioms have not been demonstrated to be true—axioms cannot be proven. Perhaps they have been described with some accuracy. Only if this is the case can we hope that what has been said might contribute a little to a better mutual understanding.

VIII

WORK AND
VOCATION

Work is one of the serious problems for twentieth–century man. Our attitude toward our work is highly ambiguous. We could say it has two sides. At times it is considered an evil and the burden of our life. Others consider it *the* good and the source of all meaning. We consider work an evil, at best a necessary evil, and we try to reduce the number of hours and years a man has to work. Now, the negative attitude toward work illustrated by this tendency to reduce the hours that people spend working, has its source in what one could call the deterioration of all work into labor. I am using here the distinction of work and labor which Hannah Arendt has made in her book, *The Human Condition*. Work is the expenditure of energy to do something or produce something for use. Labor is production for consumption.

A man who builds a table or a chair—a cabinetmaker—works. A person who manufactures Kleenex labors. The strange thing that has happened in the twentieth century is that there is less and less production for use, and more and more production for consumption. People do not make things to last, but to break down. This is known in the trade as built–in obsolescence, and strangely enough and depressingly enough, if it were not so, we would all starve. This built–in obsolescence is a necessary part of our kind of industrial society. It is because people want new cars that we have prosperity, and if people do not buy new cars we have a recession. But people will buy new cars only if the old cars are no longer what they want, if they are obsolete. Thus to build cars that will soon be obsolete is necessary in order to have prosperity. But this character of the product gives the person engaged in the process of production a feeling that he is not doing anything worthwhile. A person who builds for use can show what he has done and can say, "I did that twenty years ago." A person who produces for consumption has no chance to have pride in his work. He labors, he does not work.

The oddest thing about this tragicomic situation is that total consumption brings total prosperity. When you have a war like World War II that destroys everything, the countries where the destruction was greatest—Germany and Japan—have had the greatest prosperity. It is almost *Alice in Wonderland*. You can see how total consumption—and war is total consumption—gives everybody a chance to produce.

The West Germans are hiring people from Greece and Italy. They are bringing in thousands and thousands of workers because although they have almost twice as many people as before World War II in a very shrunken part of their country, they do not have enough laborers; the same thing is true in Japan. Total consumption results in total production, but the result is that people feel that what they are doing does not mean anything. They are dissatisfied. They have very little pride in their work. Quality control becomes a major issue. Quality control is one of the technical terms for the fact that when you produce for consumption things will be done very sloppily. It is cheaper to discard some of the products at some point in the quality control process than to insist on perfection. The remedy to all this, as I indicated earlier, is the reduction of labor, late start, early retirement, a shorter work week, and a shorter work day.

But as I said, we have an ambiguous attitude toward work. We also think it is good. In fact, one could say that for many people work is the source of all meaning in their lives. Both attitudes are occasionally found simultaneously in the same person.

You may remember a book written a number of years ago by William H. Whyte, Jr., called *The Organization Man.* Here you have a person who has completely subordinated himself to the job. Everything in his life—the person he marries, the family, the home—is subordinated to his work. His supreme loyalty is to his job, or perhaps more accurately, to the organization which gives him his job. Mr. Whyte carried this analysis through, not only to the young executives in the major companies, but to some young seminarians, and strangely enough, even there it worked. They were also organizational men, in this sense. The reason for the importance of work is that our status in twentieth-century America depends to a very large extent on the work we do.

We are what our work is, or, in other words, our work is the focus of our identification. In other societies and other cultures, you have classes. There is the nobility; there is the bourgeoisie; there is a proletariat. We do not really have such classes. I know some of my sociologist friends say we do, but they have not been part of those societies where they *really* do. We have a highly mobile society. We have status, but you can change status, and the instrument by which you change status is essentially the job you have. Your status does not really depend on your family, whether your father, grandfather, great–grandfather belonged to a certain family. This makes a great deal of difference in Europe. In our country, status depends very largely on the kind of job you have. People try to get into jobs with high status because they feel that "You are what your job is." This is more important than family, race, religion—than any other focus of identification.

If this is the case, and to a certain degree it is the case, then you have to consider the fact that the loss of your job is the greatest disaster that can happen to you, and retirement is a major shock which becomes for many people a potential and actual disaster. Now let me repeat: I have said that our attitude toward work, toward our profession, is very ambiguous. On the one hand it is an evil, on the other hand a good. We want to be retired and we fear retirement. I would suspect that in the course of a single day each of us expresses both feelings. You say, "I wish I were somewhere on a desert island lying in the sun doing nothing," and then on the same day you feel that what you are doing is the most important thing in the world, and you would not exchange places with anybody. The strange thing is that the same person expresses both attitudes. Of course, there are some people who tend more in one direction, some who tend more in the other; but what is fascinating is that the same person combines aspects of both attitudes.

It is my claim that these attitudes have theological antecedents in our culture. We have in our Western culture a tradition usually associated with the Middle Ages, having strong biblical roots, which depreciates physical work because it is not the most important thing that man can do. Most of you may be familiar with the story in the gospel according to St. Luke, about Mary and Martha. If you are like most Americans, you do not like the story because you feel that it is embarrassing and perhaps should not be in the Bible. We hear of two women, one who works and one who just sits and listens, and Jesus praises the "un-American" one—the one who just sits and listens. This is one of those stories in the Bible that give most people in our particular culture trouble, because contemplation is not really our strength. The tendency just to sit down and think about important things, good things, is, however, part of the tradition of the West. It comes to us by way of the Greeks. Aristotle said, "Any occupation, art, science which makes the body or soul or mind of the freeman less fit for the practice or exercise of virtue, is vulgar. Wherefore, we call all those arts vulgar which tend to deform the body and likewise all paid employment, for they absorb and degrade the mind. Anybody who does anything for pay is by this very act not truly a free person." This tradition is part of our education.

Liberal arts education, in order to be truly liberal arts, is always assumed to prepare you for something which has no practical utility. The ideal of the liberal arts college is to teach that which cannot be sold, which has no saleable value. I used to teach philosophy at a small liberal arts college. Philosophy was *the* prestige subject, because nobody can do anything with philosophy except teach it again. In business parlance this is "conspicuous consumption." You spend your time doing something which you can not sell. It has no functional value. What do you do when you have a major in philosophy? Study more philosophy. This is all you can do with it, and the liberal arts ideal always tends in this direction. This Aristotelian, medieval concern is with truth and understanding; whether it is economically useful or not is a very, very secondary concern.

Utility is not really important. Those of us who are committed to this particular notion, of course, always point out that most truly useful discoveries have come from people who have had this attitude. I never tire of repeating that Heisenberg, Planck, Jung, and Einstein were all products of those highly ornamental liberal arts schools. Heisenberg was a classics major. There is something very creative in this approach, and it is clearly part of our tradition: a very negative view of any kind of work that is done for profit, for pay. Any kind of manual labor is considered not very valuable.

But we have a second tradition in the West in which work is glorified and the job is seen as source of all meaning. This

is emphasized by what one can call loosely, although in-
accurately, the "Protestant–Puritan tradition." Sociologists,
like Max Weber and H. Tawney, have claimed that there is
a tendency in later Protestantism to identify your *calling* in
this world with your *calling* from God to such a degree that
you completely serve God in your job. The idea developed
somewhat like this: God will bless his people in their work.
If you are blessed in your work, God loves you. To be sure
that God loves you, you have to prove that you are blessed
in your work. There is an easy and objective way of show-
ing how blessed in your work you are, namely, your income.
Finally you have this, in my judgment, sick notion, that the
rich are the good and the poor are the evil. If you doubt me,
a good many of our contemporary self–help books combine
success and goodness in this strange way. They claim that
if you become a religious person then you will also become
a success in your job. It is hard to understand how this can
come out of a Christian tradition, because as we all realize
Jesus, who had some standing in the Christian tradition, did
not exactly end as president of the Chamber of Commerce
of Jerusalem. There are really reasons which indicate that
this identification lacks support in the Bible, but a great
many people, nevertheless, as well as many popular best-
sellers, identify success and goodness.

This is where we stand now. We are all involved in the
ambiguity. This does not mean Protestants are on one side
and Catholics on the other, but that we are all involved in
a clash of traditions in this highly mobile society in which
we constantly learn from each other, where you have Chinese Smorgasbord and Norwegian Pizza. We are heirs of
both of these traditions.

Now added to this is a further complicating factor. Being
Americans, we have the greatest choice in the selection of
our vocations of any people in the history of mankind. As a
result, students postpone their decisions about what they

want to be and it gets later and later before they can make up their minds. To go to school seems to be the only thing they know how to do; so they go a little longer. Now in the culture from which I come there was no problem; you always were what your father was. My father was a minister; my grandfather was a minister; my great–grandfather was a minister. There was no vocational choice in this sense. In other families you were a butcher or you were a carpenter or you were a lawyer. Your family determined your vocational choice so clearly that you had to be very independent to do something else. Then you come to America. You find here a very different situation. It is a tremendous burden for American young people to be confronted by virtually five hundred options. All these things they could possibly be, and they have no real clear–cut device by which they can tell what to choose. There are some psychological aids, but they are not very good. So what are you going to do? It is a very serious problem, for this is such a crucial choice and it produces such tremendous anxieties because of the variety of possibilities available and the fear of making the wrong decision. Add to this the lack of a clear philosophy or a clear idea of what we really want which might guide us in making this choice. You see why we are confused. Most Americans shuttle between doing what is right and doing what makes money. The ideal is to combine the two. Most of us, however, have these spurts in which we feel that making money is not important at all. What is really important is doing what is right. This is why such an endeavor as a Peace Corps can be a success; because all sorts of people really want to do what they deeply feel is right. But it is not clear how they can accomplish it.

This ambivalence toward work and the resulting uncertainty and anxiety are part of the situation of the last quarter of the twentieth century. I think we have to learn to live with them. I am not saying there is a pat solution to this dichotomy, but I would like to suggest a few guiding principles which might enable us to live with this ambiguity —the clash between work as good and work as evil.

The first principle I would suggest is professional competence. To the degree that you know your work and can perform it well, you are less subject to stress caused by the ambiguities I have described. This means you may still have real doubts. Let me be specific and take a situation that must sometimes face people in the medical profession. Sometimes you have real doubts about whether the expenditure of work for people who are bound to die two weeks later in spite of all your work, whose life in these two weeks is only a medical concept of life, is worthwhile. Is this a theological concept of life? Are you keeping a person alive or only a cancer? The question becomes very difficult. You might have real doubts about the ultimate significance of what you are doing. Now I think if you acquire satisfaction in proximate efficiency, it gives you stability even if you have doubts about the ultimate meaning. There is real satisfaction in doing something very well, even if you have doubts, justifiable doubts, about its ultimate significance. I think this is true of many professions, almost all of them. There are always borderline areas in which you really do not know whether what you are doing is ultimately significant. But by doing your job well, by having professional competence, you can get some meaning out of it, though it does not solve the ultimate problem.

The second thing I call professional seriousness. I do not know if you have read Mark Twain's story about the time he went to a watchmaker because his watch had stopped. He had forgotten to wind it. Now he had wound it again and he wanted to set it according to the watchmaker's clock. The watchmaker took it out of his hand, looked at it, and, declaring that it was slow, proceeded to "fix" it. From that day on Mark Twain took it from one watchmaker to another but the watch never worked right again. It was useless from the day he had taken it to this first watchmaker. Mark Twain ends his story with the remark, "and I used to wonder what became of all the unsuccessful tinkers, gunsmiths, showmakers, and blacksmiths. But nobody could ever tell me."

You have here the story of the Jack–of–all–trades. One of the wonders of the frontier has become one of the curses of a developed America. On the frontier, you had to be a Jack–of–all–trades because there was not anybody else around to do it better. But we have glorified the Jack–of–all–trades to the point where all of us, instead of getting somebody who knows his business, try to do all sorts of things we cannot do very well. The result is a sort of Jack–of–all–trades attitude toward the professions.

I will take the teaching profession as an example. Many people teach as a side-line after the children are grown or for other reasons of this kind. Since they are not serious about teaching, they have no professional pride. It is a job they do to make some money on the side. But this attitude negatively affects the entire teaching profession.

I am afraid the same problem might threaten other professions. We have to have a serious professional attitude otherwise the significance of our work is undercut. We undercut it ourselves if we are not serious about what we are doing. And if we are not serious why should anybody else be? If we consider it a part–time affair which we can take up and drop repeatedly as we feel like it, why should anybody else consider it a full–time profession? If we think that it can be done in a sort of off–hand manner with part of our mind, while the important part of our mind is concentrated elsewhere, why should we expect anybody else to take it seriously? I think this is the Jack–of–all–trades attitude which we have in many fields where all sorts of jobs are done by people who have no real qualification.

Even the ministry has this problem. You know I can start a church tomorrow, call it the true church of George Forell, and if some are gullible enough to join, we have a new denomination. There are no professional standards. Anybody can call himself "reverend" and ordain other people. I have known "bishops" whose only memberships were their families. Who is going to stop them from calling themselves bishop? All of us have problems in this Jack–of–all–trades tradition. We have a serious problem that is a result of this frontier attitude, justified at the time, but dangerous today. This is what I meant by the need for professional seriousness.

I have two more observations. We have to be aware of the reality of law in the theological sense. We live in a structured universe in which life is lived according to laws that are a part of life itself and that cannot be changed. We ought to accept unpretentiously the "givenness" of life and thus be preserved from taking ourselves too seriously. In medicine, in ministering, in teaching, there is this tendency. We assume that we are God, which we are not, thank God. You heard the story about the self–made man about whom it was said that he was a living testimony to the dangers of unskilled labor. This tendency to take ourselves too seriously is so dangerous because it paralyzes us. We are paralyzed from doing what we may be able to do because we try to do what we cannot. Teachers are not always successful. Doctors are not always successful. Ministers are not always successful. Sometimes they are successful in spite of everything they have done. Some people survived in the eighteenth century in spite of the medical profession, which bled everybody, trying to get rid of bad humors.

Somehow this is a universe not of our own making and we should not act as if it were of our own making. Whether you believe in God or not, this absolute belief in man is destructive of the possibilities we have because we put too much of the burden on somebody who cannot carry it. We did not make this world; it is subject to universal law which will go on with or without us, with or without mankind. It is God's universe, not ours.

This brings me to a final observation. We ought to be aware of the reality of grace. This is another theological concept. Let me try to describe it very simply. Grace is something very much like sleep. One of the great blessings for human beings is the ability to sleep. But you all know that sleep comes to us not because we want to sleep, but because we have worked a long, hard day and then it suddenly overcomes us and we sleep. This reality of grace means that we have to learn to let go. I do not know if you have had the following experience, but I have had it many times. Something very important was going to happen the next day and I wanted to get a good night's rest. I usually sleep like a log. But under those circumstances I can make a major production of it. I take a warm bath; I really go to bed early, and I constantly say to myself that I must get some sleep, it is very important. I must go to sleep, and I am wide awake. The harder I try to go to sleep, the more awake I remain.

I think this illustrates this passivity of man, this receptiveness of man that is necessary for living a life out of grace. This means one must learn to let go. Some people have what I like to call a pan–ethical approach. They try to make a production out of everything. There is not a situation which they do not blow up into a life and death matter. As a result, nothing gets done. There is a necessity in a profession to let go, to be passive, or, to say it theologically —to commit it to God—to say I've done so much and that it is all I can do. To try to do more ruins you and then ruins the people you work with. This is true in the relationship of people to each other. One needs the ability to let go, the ability to forget an issue instead of making one. One needs the ability not to see things. It is God who sees all things, we do not have to.

There are situations in relationships to children in which inaction is the wisest course. A mother sometimes does not hear the shouting of her offspring, and by not hearing it she solves the problem. When her children are fighting, if the mother becomes involved the solution may become more difficult. But if she just does not hear them they may manage to settle the argument themselves. Now I admit it is a very difficult thing to know when you have to act and when you do not have to intervene. The point I would like to make is that there is no virtue in scrupulosity. There is no virtue in trying to make every conflict into a major issue, in trying to solve everything. "Sufficient unto the day is the evil thereof." Do not borrow trouble. But in this world many people believe that they are Atlas who upholds the world, that if they close their eyes for just a minute, the world is going to collapse into nothingness. In this kind of a world, people cannot sleep because they cannot let go. I think we have to recover the sense that God's grace upholds and maintains us always, in order that we may do our job, not neurotically, but faithfully.

IX

THE
DEVELOPMENT OF AN ECOLOGIC
CONSCIENCE

The perversion of the best is the worst. Only in areas where we are talented can we cause real damage. It is the truly beautiful girl who can drive men to die for her. This is the story of Helen of Troy. Had Helen been a more ordinary, more homely woman, Hector and Achilles and thousands of Greeks and Trojans would not have died so tragically in the great Trojan War.

Had Adolph Hitler been a less charismatic personality, unable to play on all the hidden complexes of the Germans, the history of the twentieth century might have been quite different. Indeed, it was the vaunted efficiency of the Germans which enabled the Nazis to exterminate millions of persons in their horribly efficient concentration camps.

It is the praiseworthy sense of Boy Scout and Rotarian morality which is responsible for America's tragic and confused involvement in the affairs of other people. Trying to do our daily good deed and trying to serve mankind according to our limited sights we have become responsible not only for My Lai but also for the corpses floating down the Mekong River with their hands tied behind their backs, victims of ancient ethnic conflicts in Indochina which we can neither understand nor abolish, but which we encouraged with our tragic, fumbling, and destructive presence.

With our naive and pervasive notion—shared by the extreme right and the extreme left—that a man can do no wrong if he thinks his heart is pure, we have developed a peculiar Midas touch. We have brought destruction and death where we hoped to bring peace and life.

The perversion of the best is the worst. The charming combination of optimism, willingness to help, and ignorance of history which makes American young people almost everywhere popular and attractive—this very combination has made us into a threat to the survival of the race. On TV, Marshall Dillon is an attractive hero in the never–never land somewhere over the rainbow in nineteenth century Dodge City, Kansas. But a nation that sees itself as a cosmic Matt Dillon is a danger to itself and others. TV's "Mission Impossible" is a sinister symbol of this development.

And our environmental crisis is as much the result of the perversion of the best as our political crisis. Our attitude toward our environment is the result of a peculiar combination of the two main sources of our morality: the Judeo–Christian tradition coming to us through the Bible; and the Apollonian–Socratic tradition coming to us from ancient Greece. This combination has served us well. The modern scientific technological world is the result of the view expressed in Genesis 1:26: "Then God said, 'Let us make man in our image, after our likeness, and let them have dominion over the fish of the sea, and over the birds of the air, over the cattle, and over all the earth, and over every creeping thing that creeps upon the earth.' So God created man in his own image, in the image of God he created them. And God blessed them, and God said to them 'Be fruitful and multiply, and fill the earth and subdue it; and have dominion over the fish of the sea and over the birds of the air and over every living thing that moves upon the earth.'"

Genesis demythologized the cosmic myths of the Canaanite neighbors of the Jews. It overthrew Baal and Baal worship and freed man for the conquest of nature. Man is believed to have the God–given right, indeed the duty to populate the earth and conquer nature. Large families and the accumulation of wealth are moral demands. Consistent with this Judeo–Christian tradition, John Wesley said, "Earn all you can, save all you can, give all you can." And in order to do this you were allowed to exploit nature which long ago had been stripped of the holiness, the sacred garment with which paganism and pantheism had protected it.

Added to this heritage from the Bible was the Apollonian heritage of the Greeks as expressed in the saying of Protagoras: "Man is the measure of all things, of things that are that they are, and of things that are not, that they are not."

This anthropocentric tradition, brilliantly articulated by Socrates and his disciples, who depreciated nature as a world of unreality and shadows and riveted man's attention to his interior world, the world of ideas, freed the West for its ruthless march that leads us across the earth and unto the moon.

Mother Earth became a mere object to be skillfully carved like a Thanksgiving turkey; nature became an impersonal slave to be used at man's pleasure. And many people naively believe that the same ruthless drive which conquered the earth will enable us to find new worlds to conquer and to throw away this, our earth, like an empty beer can as we take off toward other planets and stars, like picnickers leaving a lake shore.

I said earlier that the perversion of the best is the worst, but you may ask what was good about all of the Christian Apollonian heritage? It abolished human sacrifices to ensure fertility, it allowed the harnessing of water and wind to serve and feed man. It produced prosperity and leisure which in turn permitted the development of a democratic culture. Literature, music, and the arts became available to all, not only to a small élite.

But granted these very real achievements, it is becoming increasingly obvious that the present development, if continued, will destroy man and his environment. The escape to other planets is a pipedream, and we will have to find ways of coming to terms with our environment to keep earth habitable for us and our children.

What ideological resources are available for such a reconstruction of Western thought?

I would like to endorse Lynn White's comments in his article "The Historical Roots of Our Ecologic Crisis."

> . . . we should ponder the greatest radical in Christian history since Christ: Saint Francis of Assisi. The prime miracle of Saint Francis is the fact that he did not end at the stake, as many of his left-wing followers did. He was so clearly heretical that a general of the Franciscan Order, Saint Bonaventura, a great and perceptive Christian, tried to suppress the early accounts of Franciscanism. The key to an understanding of Francis is his belief in the virtue of humility—not merely for the individual but for man as a species. Francis tried to depose man from his monarchy over creation and set up a democracy for all God's creatures. With him the ant is no longer simply a homily for the lazy, flames a sign of the thrust of the soul toward union with God; now they are Brother Ant and Sister Fire, praising the Creator in their own ways as Brother Man does in his.
>
> Later commentators have said that Francis preached to the birds as a rebuke to men who would not listen. The records do not read so: he urged the little birds to praise God, and in spiritual ecstasy they flapped their wings and chirped rejoicing. Legends of saints, especially the Irish saints, had long told of their dealings with animals but always, I believe, to show their human dominance over creatures. With Francis it is different. The land around Gubbio in the Apennines was being ravaged by a fierce wolf. Saint Francis, says the legend, talked to the wolf and persuaded him of the error of his ways. The wolf repented, died in the odor of sanctity, and was buried in consecrated ground.
>
> What Sir Steven Ruciman calls "the Franciscan doctrine of the animal soul" was quickly stamped out. Quite possibly it was in part inspired, consciously or unconsciously, by the belief in reincarnation held by the Cathar heretics who at that time teemed in Italy and southern France, and who presumably had got it originally from India. It is significant that at just the same moment, about 1200, traces of metem-

psychosis are found also in Western Judaism, in the Provencal CABBALA. But Francis held neither to transmigration of souls nor to pantheism. His view of nature and of man rested on a unique sort of panpsychism of all things animate and inanimate, designed for the glorification of their transcendent Creator, who, in the ultimate gesture of cosmic humility, assumed flesh, lay helpless in a manger, and hung dying on a scaffold.

I am not suggesting that many contemporary Americans who are concerned about our ecologic crisis will be either able or willing to counsel with wolves or exhort birds. However, the present increasing disruption of the global environment is the product of a dynamic technology and science which were originating in the Western medieval world against which Saint Francis was rebelling in so original a way. Their growth cannot be understood historically apart from distinctive attitudes toward nature which are deeply grounded in Christian dogma. The fact that most people do not think of these attitudes as Christian is irrelevant. No new set of basic values has been accepted in our society to displace those of Christianity. Hence we shall continue to have a worsening ecologic crisis until we reject the Christian axiom that nature has no reason for existence save to serve man.[1]

In the words of Joseph Sittler, Jr. of the University of Chicago, we will have to learn to see nature as our sister and protect her from those who would ravish her. Nobody has the right to poison the water and the air, be it ever so profitable. You would not let anybody sell your sister into prostitution just because it might be profitable. Why should we let anybody poison the earth, the water, the air, just because it is their way of earning a living? Nobody has the inalienable right to poison anybody!

And this brings me to a second resource for a new ethics. Albert Schweitzer articulated it a generation ago in his *Philosophy of Civilization* and called it "reverence for life."

[1] Lynn White, Jr., "The Historical Roots of Our Ecologic Crisis" *Science* (Vol. 155, March 10, 1967), pp. 1203–1207. Copyright © 1967 by the American Association for the Advancement of Science. Reprinted with the permission of the publisher and the author.

He said, "Ethics is responsibility without limit towards all that lives."[2] Schweitzer said, "We are afraid of making ourselves conspicuous if we let it be noticed how we feel for the sufferings which man brings upon the animals. At the same time we think that others have become more 'rational' than we are, and regard what we are excited about as usual and a matter of course. Yet suddenly they will let slip a word which shows that they have not yet learned to acquiesce. And now, though they were strangers, they are quite near us. The mask in which we deceived each other falls off."[3] The masks must fall, we must quit playing the games of unconcern. Trying to be unperturbed, we will make it too destructive for all of us. Reverence for all life is the condition for continued human life. Life turns out to be indivisible. Only responsibility toward all life will preserve your life and mine.

And finally I would like to call your attention to a third resource toward an ethic of survival, Martin Buber's *I and Thou*. He saw human history as a progressive augmentation of the world of It. He observed that "the eternal Thou can by its nature not become It." What he suggests and what I would like to suggest to you is to recover the Thou in man *and* in nature. The flower and the tree, the river and the mountain that has become a Thou to you is a glimpse through to the eternal Thou. We must not try to escape from the world to God but rather we must learn to see all of the world as a symbol of God, participating in the reality toward which it points. We must try to overcome the ever–increasing power of the It which sucks away our life and our hope and learn to sing again with the Psalmist: "The heavens declare the glory of God and the firmament showeth his handiwork" (Ps. 19:1).

---

[2] Albert Schweitzer, *The Philosophy of Civilization* (New York: Macmillan, 1949), p. 311.

[3] *Ibid.*, p. 319.

X

LAW AND
GOSPEL AS A PROBLEM
OF POLITICS

If one would define the crucial problem of the sixteenth century as the problem of faith and the crucial problem of the eighteenth century as the problem of truth, it could be said that the crucial problem of the twentieth century is the problem of politics.

The decisive question on which everything depended for sixteenth-century man was the decision between contending religious forces. Later, the all–important question became the attitude toward the supremacy of reason and the truths which reason can supply over all values and standards. It has been left to the twentieth century to place the state and man's political decisions in the center of his existence.

The open conflicts of our age are not religious, if religion is to be understood as relating man directly to God, and they are not in the realm of knowledge and science. All these matters are now subordinated to politics. Right, orthodox, wise, and true is the man who holds the accepted political view, even though everything else about him may be questionable. He may have the wrong religion—or no religion at all. He may be ignorant or untruthful. If he shares our political opinions, he is acceptable. Whether we realize it or not, the political problem has become the central problem of our life.

Yet in spite of this pivotal position of politics in our life it is not easy to establish the relationship of the Christian faith to this concern. Actually, one could say that the three most prevalent ways in which Christendom relates itself to politics in our time are all perverse and sterile.

First we have those who claim that Christianity is irrelevant to politics. The realm of politics has its own laws. It is the realm of power, and all political action is the result of the actual constellation of power. In politics we do what we have the power to do, and all other claims are merely ornamentation. People may label their decisions as Christian, but that is merely for purposes of propaganda. It may be the Christian's duty, as some say, to refuse to build, stock, or use atomic weapons. It may be his duty, as others say, to advocate the building, stockpiling, and if need be, use of these same arms. Theologians may debate these questions with great agitation, but that is merely their particular idea of a good time. Whatever they decide will make as much difference to the actions that will eventually be taken as a debate among natural scientists concerning the good or evil effect of sunspots on human life. Just as the sunspots will come and go whether scientists have declared them useful or harmful, so atomic weapons will be used if the power constellation permits it, regardless of the condemnation or endorsement of theologians.

In this analysis of the relationship of Christianity and politics, the moral exhortations of theologians and the value judgments of the churches are considered purely decorative. They have nothing whatsoever to do with the actual process of decision–making. Religion, in general, and Christianity, in particular, are considered irrelevant to the power struggle that makes up political life.

While this attitude is perhaps not often openly accepted in our society, it is the hidden assumption among many practitioners in the field of politics. They are prepared to render lip-service to religious ideals to adorn their argument, but they are sure that Christianity is irrelevant to the actual process of arriving at political decisions.

A second attitude, widely represented in America, sees Christianity as sentimentality in politics. It is the disregard of relevant facts in the process of making decisions in favor of arbitrarily selected criteria of special concern to one or the other Christian community. Christian considerations in politics are here those which deal, for example, with the type of beverage which the candidate drinks with his meals. His political qualifications are greatly enhanced should he not drink the beverage frowned upon by the Christian group. This fairly marginal qualification for public office will often be very highly stressed; in Germany in the 1930's faithful church members belonging to the more pietistic groups within the state church would wax eloquent in their praise of Adolf Hitler's well-known refusal to drink or to smoke.

Similarly, the size of a candidate's family or his marital status has become a consideration which apparently, in the minds of many Christian voters, outweighs most other considerations. Pictures of the candidate and his smiling wife and children serve to convince Christians that he is the man for the job he is seeking. Consideration of his family life is used to establish his ability as governor of the state or judge of the court or representative in Congress. Granted that a certain correlation between a man's success as a father and his success in public office might exist (which, however, cannot fairly be based on the looks or size of the family on a campaign poster), this presumed correlation is vastly exaggerated by Christian sentimentality. The record shows how frequently Christianity in politics has been sentimentality in politics. The justified Christian concern in the proper functioning of political life has become so skewed by irrelevant sentimentality as to make it more of a hindrance than a help. As a result, the influence of the Christian faith upon the political scene has often been marginal and weird. Christians have frequently backed the right candidate for the wrong reasons. As a result of their preoccupation with sentimental and marginal concerns, their influence on policy formulation in domestic and foreign politics has been unpredictable and inconsistent.

A third attitude, not infrequent in America, associates Christianity with reaction in politics. Christians are believed to be defenders of the *status quo*. Their activities in politics will be reactionary. This situation has been expressed in England with the slogan that the Church of England is the Conservative party at prayer. It could be translated into the American idiom by asserting that the Lutheran church is the right-wing of the Republican party at prayer.

And it seems undeniable that the church as an institution has tended to be reactionary, in spite of persistent individual voices who have challenged her to a more radical prophetic witness. All the great political changes in Western culture have come about in a peculiarly ambiguous manner. They are in a sense the result of the Christian proclamation; they are rooted in this proclamation and take their persuasive power from it; yet when these great changes were actually upon us, the church as an institution tended to drag its institutional feet and failed to supply the leadership and encouragement which one could have expected. A few illustrations might help to clarify this point.

When slavery was a great political and social issue in this country, the voice of the major Christian churches was oddly muffled. Surely, some of the major abolitionists were motivated by Christian ideals. Such groups as the Quakers had abolished slavery in their own ranks a century earlier. Yet, by and large, it must be said that the institutional church tried to avoid the issue as long as possible and used a quite pitiful exegesis of the Old Testament (Gen. 9:20–28) in order to justify the retention of the *status quo*.

Other illustrations are numerous. In the fight for justice for women, justice for labor, social security, etc., we find this peculiar foot–dragging, this odd ambiguity of the position of the Christian church. Although today the record of the mainstream of the Christian community in the race issue in America is better than past experience would have led us to expect, it is certainly still far too ambiguous. If we take into account places like South Africa, it is sometimes truly shameful. For those of us who do not share this common Christian conservatism it is not easy to understand how the Christian impulses for justice and reform, which, as we said, undergird almost all our advances, could become so independent from the institutional church. It should be noted that by becoming separated from the soil which made them grow they not only weakened the church, which had nourished them, but in turn became distorted and sometimes actually perverse (prohibitionism, Communism, feminist chauvinism, etc.)—a threat to the very healing they were trying to foster.

In review, it must be said that the relationship between Christianity and politics in our civilization has not been a constructive one. The Christian proclamation should not be irrelevant to political life, it should not be reactionary. To avoid these pitfalls the methodological distinction between law and gospel may be of service.

THE CHRISTIAN ASSERTION OF THE LAW

Nowhere is law more necessary than in the realm of politics. We define law as "the principle and operation of order in the world." Where so many different and opposing interests meet, as in the area of politics, some principle of order is essential for the preservation of life. Indeed, this has been so clearly discerned by all those who have given the problem any thought that their eagerness to establish order at any price has not infrequently led them to the advocacy of tyranny. The Christian faith offers a number of insights from its particular understanding of law and gospel which might, if accepted, contribute substantially to the welfare of man in the body politic.

The universality of law

The Christian church on the basis of God's revelation in
Holy Scripture proclaims the universality of law. All men
everywhere and at all times are under the law. This law
may be the revealed law of the Old Testament or the law
written in the hearts of man of which the Apostle Paul
speaks. ("They show that what the law requires is written
on their hearts." Rom. 2:15)

There are indeed vast differences in the positive law as
we discover it in the various human societies. These differences are fascinating and impressive (cf. Ruth Benedict,
Patterns of Culture), but for the Christian they all express
more or less adequately the fact that man everywhere is
confronted by a structure not of his own making. It is impossible to speak of "lesser breeds without the law," and
this type of speech, whether uttered from Christian arro-
gance or pagan relativism, merely confuses the issue.

But if the law is universal this means that it is possible to
create political community. Because of this fact we can enforce laws equitably in our town, if we so desire, and eventually may be able to enforce law equitably in the entire
world. It is simply not true that laws are merely the will of
those who are powerful oppressing those who are weak. Of
course, there is an element of truth in this observation. The
law as administered in the world is perverted by the fact of
sin. Justice is not as blind as we would like to believe—
rather frequently it appears to be crosseyed. But when all
this has been said, the fact remains that this is a perversion
of justice and understood as a perversion by everybody,
even the very people who do the perverting. It may happen
that an influential politician can bend the law to his purposes, but we know that this is not the intrinsic fault of the
principle of law but rather the fault of inadequate law
enforcement.

By its insistence upon the universality of law the Christian church accepts a basis for cooperation with all those who share this respect for law. This means in the realm of politics it is possible to obtain a modicum of cooperation between peoples separated by fundamental theological differences on the basis of their common acceptance of law. In domestic politics this may mean that a Christian might cooperate with an atheistic labor leader or a businessman who happens to be an adherent of the Bahai cult for certain limited political objectives, provided these objectives are in conformity to law according to the insights of all three. It is not of central importance for the achievement of the limited objectives whether the others are theologically properly motivated. This is indeed ultimately important for their sake, but it should not be made the condition for cooperation for limited political and social objectives. It is sheer nonsense to insist that we must have a subscription to the Lutheran Confessions from every member of the PTA before we are going to sign their petition for police protection of the children at a busy street-crossing. It is sufficient that we know that our action is the fruit of our faith and does not compromise it. The same insight holds true for international cooperation. Here, too, action on the basis of law and for the achievement of limited objectives is possible, even though no ultimate unity of faith exists. The source of such cooperation is the universality of law as experienced by all men.

The absoluteness of law

On the basis of biblical revelation we are forced to say not only that the law is universal but also that it is absolute. In other words, the structure which confronts us is not arbitrary or freely reversible. There are, of course, laws of this nature. The law that requires us to drive on the right-hand side of the road is arbitrary. If we had a law telling us all to drive on the left it would be equally acceptable. To drive on the right-hand side is not intrinsically better than to drive on the left. However, to demand a law which should regulate traffic in a country with the traffic density of the United States is not a matter of moral indifference. This is an absolute demand of justice, deriving its strength from the universally accepted notion that we should do unto others as we would like them to do unto us. It is a "norm of action which reason discovers by examination of the functional order that exists objectively in the nature of man and his relation to other men and the external world."[1] The absoluteness of law is based upon the fact that such norms of action are discernible in spite of the perversions brought about by man's sin.

We don't know how it came about that if you give three apples to six people they feel they should each get one half an apple. Or that even the aborigines after a few days in London will understand that to stand in line waiting for the bus is a reasonable and equitable solution to the problem of too many passengers and too few buses. Chickens never seem to get this point; human beings generally do. The fact that some apparently never do does not invalidate the general rule. The soundness of certain essential principles of equity is discoverable by all people. These principles are not arbitrary or reversible (e.g., honesty) and thus establish the absoluteness of the law.

What does all this imply for the realm of politics? It suggests that political life must be so organized as to give the greatest amount of support to these norms of action. Thus, "Rulers are not a terror to good conduct, but to bad. Would you have no fear of him who is in authority? Then do what is good, and you will receive his approval" (Rom. 13:3). This description of government by the Apostle Paul is the criterion of all government. The objective of the state and of politics is the earthly welfare of man. This goal can-

[1] Martin J. Hillenbrand, *Power and Morals* (New York: Columbia University Press, 1949), p. 83.

not be achieved if these "norms of action which reason discovers by examination of the functional order that exists objectively in the nature of man and his relation to other men and to the external world" are ignored.

This means that the Christian must insist that the undergirding principles, which are to be expressed in all positive laws and established and enforced by means of politics, are absolute. He cannot operate arbitrarily with the notion that any law is good. Rather he must distinguish between those positive laws which support the absolute norms of action and those which are irrelevant to them or may even subvert them. Again he will be able to cooperate with non–Christians in the practical affairs of political life, since the norms of action for politics are by their nature reasonable and will appeal to reasonable men. If one nation has a great surplus of food which depresses prices and endangers the prosperity of its people, it should be possible to persuade even convinced non–Christians that it would be reasonable to give away the surpluses to people who are hungry and could use them. If slums are shown to breed crime, it should be possible to bring about slum clearance with the help of all reasonable men in order to achieve the universally desirable goal of reducing the incidence of crime.

Of course, the Christian knows that reason is a tool which is perverted by sin, that people are not guided by reason alone but by all sorts of irrational and antirational drives. Yet he will use the norms reason discovers to check and balance these drives. He will also utilize these very same irrational drives for the sake of achieving what he knows to be in man's interest on the basis of the law. But since the Christian is man and not God, he may be in error; he will be perverted by his own sin and thus will have innumerable difficulties in his pursuit of the law. But he must, nevertheless, pursue it. For he knows that universal and absolute law is ultimately rooted in God's will for man and the world. It is a means which God has established to preserve order and to restrain the self–destructive tendencies of sin while the church is waiting for the final consummation. This is the political use of the law, and the Christian church has the duty to make use of the law in this sense in order to contribute to the earthly welfare of man.

As it is the duty of the Christian to feed the hungry and to visit the sick, it is his duty to do everything in his power to contribute to the earthly welfare of man by political means. Especially in a democracy this responsibility is obvious. And the Lord will hold us no less responsible for our failures to use our political opportunity to serve the neighbor than for our failures to serve him through the neighbor in the more obvious forms: "I was hungry and you gave me food, I was thirsty and you gave me drink, I was a stranger and you welcomed me, I was naked and you clothed me, I was sick and you visited me, I was in prison and you came to me" (Matt. 25:35–36). Indeed this description covers practically every constructive political activity which we might undertake. It implies concern with slums and education, health and immigration. For Christians, it is not optional to bring the insights of the law to bear upon the political life; it is their Christian duty.

THE CHRISTIAN ASSERTION OF THE GOSPEL

But how about the relationship of the gospel to the realm of politics? Does the proclamation of God's love and forgiveness in Jesus Christ have anything to do with this complex of problems? The answer to this question is not easy. Obviously the gospel of Jesus Christ cannot be a resource in the political life of men in the same manner in which the law represents such a resource. An overwhelming majority of the people of the world neither know nor believe the gospel. For this reason alone it cannot be the basis for cooperation with non–Christians, and it cannot undergird politics. Arguments based upon our knowledge of God's love revealed in Jesus Christ, his Cross, and his Resurrection will not impress or persuade all those who either do not believe this deed of God at all or render it only lip service. In our dealings with our non–Christian neighbors here in the United States and all over the world we must be careful not to base political cooperation upon the gospel. For not only can the gospel not supply such a basis for those who do not believe it, but as the message of God's kingdom invading our world it proclaims a rule which we cannot establish with our own resources. "Thy kingdom come"; but what is meant by this petition? "The kingdom of God comes indeed of itself, without our prayer, but we pray in this petition that it may come unto us also." (Luther's *Small Catechism*).

To try to establish the kingdom of God out of our own power goes straight against Christ's words, "My kingdom is not of this world" (John 18:36). The effort to establish God's kingdom by means of human power is a blasphemous attempt to accomplish what God alone can effect. Whenever men have claimed to establish the kingdom of God upon earth in this manner, they have turned the gospel into law, and the actual political order has been tyrannical and by its arrogant assumptions frequently more like the kingdom of Satan. Witches have been burned, heretics persecuted, crusades fought, freedom suppressed, justice perverted—and all this in the name of the Prince of Peace. As Dostoevsky has so brilliantly shown in the story of the Grand Inquisitor, the establishment by men of such a kingdom must needs lead again to the crucifixion of the Christ in whose name this alleged kingdom of God upon earth has been established.

But does all this mean that the gospel is irrelevant to the problems of politics? The answer to this question should be a categorical No! Through the Christian Church and the Christian believer, as the leaven leavening the loaf and the light shining in the darkness, the gospel of Christ will exert an indirect but important influence upon the political life of the community.

The universality of the gospel

It is therefore important to remember that for Christians this gospel is universally relevant. The fact that God is the Father of our Lord Jesus Christ, that he loves us and wants to save us, will influence the Christian also in his political dealings. It is as a forgiven sinner that he participates in the political life. This will protect him against false hopes and false despair.

Knowing about sin in its pervasiveness and subtlety the Christian participates in politics with fewer illusions concerning the possibilities of political achievement and greater realism concerning the ambiguities of political life. He knows that there is no political solution to the human predicament; no political decision can extricate man from his involvement in sin. As a Christian he will reject the claims of contending political forces that they have the ability to abolish the evil that has always threatened man's existence. He will reject the utopian hopes that are offered from all sides and which promise to abolish man's difficulties but in fact threaten to abolish man. The knowledge that God's deed in Jesus Christ alone can save should make the Christian immune to the siren songs of all sorts of political and social saviors. Thus the gospel is a source of cool and calm realism in the political turmoil and fanaticism of our age.

Simultaneously, the very same gospel will also safeguard the Christian against the equally tempting false despair which threatens to overwhelm modern man as he tries to engage in politics. A great many of our contemporaries who have lost faith in the utopias of yesterday which were to

establish perfect justice are now convinced the "futopia"—
the *Brave New World* of Huxley or the *1984* of George
Orwell—is to be the fate of man. According to them, we are
being driven toward this futopia by an inexorable fate, and
every effort to avoid this political hell only hastens the day
of its coming.

Against this despair, which characterizes so much of the
political thinking of contemporary intellectuals, the Christian depends again on the resources of the gospel. In the
means of grace God offers him the forgiveness of sins which
alone can enable him to act courageously and confidently in
the midst of the ambiguities of public life. Of course, he
will not escape sin; his actions in the realm of politics will
involve him in injustice, pride, and all sorts of evil. But even
"though devils all the world should fill, all seeking to devour
us; we tremble not, we fear no ill, they shall not overpower
us." The gospel frees the Christian *from* despair and *for*
responsible and intelligent action in the realm of politics.
Because he knows of the forgiveness of sins, the sins which
do surround him in the life of politics cannot frighten him
into inaction and despair. Thus for the Christian the gospel,
far from being irrelevant to politics, becomes the chief resource for his political life.

And the church as the company of the cross in her communal life can and should demonstrate to the world the
power of the gospel in the realm of politics. She can and
should overcome for those who claim the name of Christ
the political divisions, national and international, which di-
vide the world. By her very existence as the communion of
the saints in which there is no East or West, no left or right,
no black or white, no class hatred or class distinction, no
iron curtain or bamboo curtain, she bears witness to the
power of the gospel in the realm of politics. Whenever we let
these political divisions split the church apart, we betray the
gospel of the Lord Jesus Christ and its universal relevance.

The absoluteness of the gospel

This very same gospel is important for the political life of man because it is absolute, the same yesterday, today, and forever. It is not subject to the changes of taste and opinion, of clime and time, which affect all human proclamations. The Christian who stands under this gospel knows that the love of God remains steadfast whatever else may change or disappear.

Into the life of politics, which by its very nature must and should be a life of give and take, of compromise and adjustment, the gospel injects for the Christian a vision of God's deed for man which should preserve him against moral surrender and the desertion of his Lord. Through the gospel, God's eternity throws its rays into human life, and this means into the area of politics as well. Even here, the Christian works *sub specie aeternitatis*. The gospel has remained the same through absolute monarchies and absolute anarchies, through all sorts of political and economic systems. It has demonstrated that not everything is merely a matter of taste or opinion. The gospel makes it manifest that there are truths one must never abandon; it is a constant reminder of that fact, and thus adds stability to the thinking of the Christian in politics. While he may not be able to explain the source of this stability to the non–Christian, he must be able to demonstrate it. Political realism must never become political opportunism, and prudential compromise must never deteriorate into moral surrender. The absoluteness of the eternal gospel should preserve the Christian from all these perversions. And should he nevertheless stumble and fall, the same gospel will raise him up again and turn him in the right direction. In the confusion of standards, the chaos of truths, the welter of voices and claims which beset him, it is the absoluteness of the gospel which supplies the personal compass.

Here again, it is the living witness of the church as the communion of saints which by its life through the ages, in spite of perversions and deviations, bears witness to this absolute gospel. The Christian individual does not stand alone; he cannot stand alone. Rather he is upheld, even in his political task, by the communion of believers who proclaim to him and to each other the eternal gospel of Jesus Christ. As a part of this body the Christian in politics is kept mindful of the absoluteness of the gospel as a personal resource in his political engagement.

The Christian proclamation should not be irrelevant to man's political life, it should not add sentimental confusion, and it should not be reactionary. It has been our claim that in order to avoid these distortions of the Christian understanding of the political task the distinction between law and gospel is of central importance. It should have become clear that this distinction does not mean that either the law or the gospel is suppressed or neglected in its application to the political life. On the contrary, both law and gospel are important for the Christian in politics. But while the law is immediately and socially relevant, the gospel is mediately and personally relevant. Through the created universality of legal structure the law's ordering power upholds the body politic. The Christian in politics should elucidate and utilize this situation. But through the Christian individual and through the Christian church as the communion of saints the saving power of the gospel penetrates the political realm, and the healing power of this gospel extends also to the men and women engaged in this controversial area of human life.

But through both, law and gospel, it is God who deals with man. Only as the church proclaims law and gospel in their common source in God and their separate and distinct functions in the world of man does she contribute her full share to the soundness of the political life of mankind.

XI

THE
CRIMINAL JUSTICE SYSTEM:
A THEOLOGICAL
PERSPECTIVE

The human need for criminal justice systems can be explained only on the basis of man's humanity, his fundamental and unique distinction from the animal. At the same time, criminal justice systems are necessary precisely because this unique and fundamental humanity has been distorted and corrupted.

Today society considers only the failures and deviations of human beings to be "crimes." It would be nonsense to speak of the "crimes" of elephants or mosquitoes, although trials of animals for alleged crimes were not uncommon until recent times. It is because we believe that man has options which enable him to make choices that we consider certain actions "criminal." Because we consider adult human beings uniquely responsible and fundamentally different from the animal, we accuse them of "crimes," try to establish the degree of their "guilt," and punish them in various ways from the imposition of fines to the withdrawal of rights, including the rights otherwise considered "inalienable," namely, life, liberty, property, and the pursuit of happiness.

This approach to human behavior assumes a certain view of man which in Western culture has been greatly influenced by the biblical tradition. From the expulsion of Adam and Eve because they ate of the "tree of the knowledge of good and evil" (Gen. 2:17) to the vision of the Book of Revelation, "Behold, I am coming soon, bringing my recompense, to repay every one for what he has done" (Rev. 22:12), the biblical view of man is informed by the notion of human responsibility. Indeed, the dramatic resolution of the tension between guilt and divine mercy in the cross of Christ and the gospel of forgiveness assumes human responsibility whether personal, collective, or a combination of both. The notions of innocence, guilt, atonement, and forgiveness are inextricably connected with the idea of justice and righteousness. The legal language used by so much of Christian theology resulted in a quasi–religious sanction for the procedures of criminal justice.

The crisis in the criminal justice system today is to a large degree a crisis in the credibility of the belief–system which undergirds our kind of justice. It has been replaced in the Western and Eastern worlds by certain "scientific" ideologies which seem to deny the reality of personal guilt. Some assert that human behavior is entirely the result of conditioning. Just as a badly trained dog may be retrained at a school where he will be reconditioned by means of reward and punishment for further usefulness, so a badly conditioned human being is reconditioned at an institution which will make him "good," which here means socially useful. If the dog or the person should prove incorrigible, he must be destroyed.

Due to the influence of Western traditions exalting human life, the untrainable offender may be placed in a mental hospital. His inability to accept "training" makes him, by definition, legally insane. This attitude is clearly indicated by the treatment of Russian intellectuals with deviant political views in the Soviet Union, and it was tried in the United States when the distinguished American poet, Ezra Pound, was placed in a mental hospital because of his objectionable political views during World War II.

In North America, however, the legal tradition has generally made a distinction between the criminally insane and criminals. The criterion is the "knowledge of good and evil." It is assumed that all those who are not criminally insane know the difference between "right" and "wrong" and are, to some degree, responsible for their actions (the McNaughton Rule).

In spite of the very serious problems which this assumption raises, the opposing view, which assumes complete environmental and hereditary determination, is even more dehumanizing in its implications. It obliterates the distinction between man and animals.

Martin Luther's opposition to any human claim to freedom in man's relationship with God is well known. He describes the human will as "bound." But even he does not side with the determinists when discussing human responsibility. Stressing the importance of the difference between men and animals at this point, he grants all men a certain freedom in regard to the world and insists that man lives simultaneously in two kingdoms.[1] In one he is guided by his own will and counsel and must make his way wisely and responsibly "without rules and mandates from God."[2] Here man rules and is lord. Although God supports man even in this realm, he does not interfere with man's freedom through specific laws. Indeed, Luther blames the "Papists" for having taken this residual freedom away and establishing all kinds of human regulations with fraudulent divine sanctions in areas where man should be free.[3]

---

[1] Martin Luther, *De Servo Arbitrio* ("On the Bondage of the Will"), 1525, by A. Freitag, ed., in *D. Martin Luthers Werke*, Kritische Gesamtausgabe, XVIII (Weimar: H. Bohlaus Nachfolger, 1908), p. 683.

[2] *Ibid.*, p. 672.

[3] *Ibid. Cf.: Calvin: Institutes of the Christian Religion*, Vol. XX of the *Library of Christian Classics*, by John T. McNeill, ed., Ford Lewis Battles, trans. (Philadelphia: Westminster Press, 1960), p. 272: ". . . since man is by nature a social animal, he tends through natural instinct to foster and preserve society. Consequently, we observe that

The biblical view of man as interpreted by Christians through the centuries posits human responsibility and the reality of guilt, including its manifestations in crime. However, the reliability of the human authorities which establish guilt and impose punishment for criminal behavior is seriously questioned. From Joseph in Egypt to John the Baptist, God's spokesmen are frequently accused of crimes and found guilty by human authorities in spite of their innocence. Though the legitimacy of the distinction between good and evil is maintained, human judges are frequently unable or unwilling to fulfill their high calling as described by St. Paul: "For government, a terror to crime, has no terrors for good behavior" (Rom. 13:3, N.E.B.). It is symptomatic of this discrepancy between the ideal and the actual that the author who provided this positive evaluation of government's administration of justice was executed in spite of his "good behavior" by the Roman government he praised.

Because sin is essentially alienation from God and the neighbor, it is not only the cause of all destructive behavior but also a disruptive power which pervades all systems of government and justice. Because the perversion of the best is generally the worst, the perversion of justice is the most profound threat to the entire system of law and government. In view of the pervasive complexity and ambiguity of the situation thus far described, certain broad recommendations will be offered for improvement in the administration of criminal justice. First, however, these preliminary considerations are in order.

It is of the greatest importance to recognize the disproportion in power and resources available to the forces of

there exist in all men's minds universal impressions of a certain civic fair dealing and order. Hence no man is to be found who does not understand that every sort of human organization must be regulated by laws, and who does not comprehend the principles of those laws. Hence arises the unvarying consent of all nations and of individual mortals with regard to laws. For their seeds have, without teacher or lawgiver, been implanted in all men.

"law and order," on the one hand, and to those persons who are most frequently accused of crimes, on the other. The prosecution has the prestige and wealth of the nation on its side, while the defendant is usually poor, ignorant, alienated, and despised. Thus the contest is very unequal, the elephant dancing among mice. For this reason, restraints protecting the mice are more important than those protecting the elephant. Because of the biblical concern for the weak, the poor, the widow, and the fatherless, it is particularly important that Christians support all attempts to balance the scales. The efforts of the United States Supreme Court to restrain the incredible power of government by requiring that it recognize certain stated rights of the accused are sound. Society must be constantly on guard against the corrupting effect of power on government.

The situation in regard to what is commonly called "organized crime" is clearly different. The justified concern of the government to restrain its power is best directed against the causes rather than the symptoms. The application of all legitimate resources of the state to crush the power of organized crime is a protection of the poor and the weak who are the most obvious and frequent victims of its pervasive and debilitating ascendancy.

But if we now look at specific problems apparent in criminal justice as it operates in North America today, it is obvious that some reasons for its malfunctioning are of a more formal nature. They are problems of design rather than content. Under this rubric belongs the overburdening of courts: with cases which should not be considered crimes at all and could be settled through other procedures; and with cases which may have been considered crimes in a homogeneous pre-pluralistic society but which can hardly be so evaluated in the context of the present situation. While Christians and adherents of other religions in our society may consider certain behavior sinful in the light of their beliefs, such behavior should not be considered criminal if disapproval is based solely on religious convictions. With reference to the preceding two categories the following causes of court congestion merit closer attention.

Accidents which are the result of life in an urban industrial society should ordinarily be adjudicated administratively rather than through courts of law (e.g., no–fault insurance). From a Christian point of view, the actual healing of the injured and the support of his dependents when an accident has occurred, whoever was at fault, seem more urgent than the dubious establishment of one party's "guilt" and the other's "innocence."

Certain types of behavior may be symptomatic of serious ills in our society and genuine expressions of man's alienation from God and neighbor. However, these should be dealt with by other means than designating them as criminal offenses. Among these acts, popularly called "crimes without victims," are gambling, public drunkenness, certain private sexual acts by consenting adults, prostitution, the possession or use of mind–altering drugs, and pornography. There are other more effective means of dealing with such socially disapproved behavior. If society wishes government to play a role, it may be in the area of education and medical treatment, rather than by means of the criminal code.

Especially since unenforced and unenforceable laws cause people to disregard and despise all law, unenforceable laws which come from a different age and no longer command the support of the majority of citizens should be deleted from the criminal code. Here belong, for example, those laws still in most state criminal codes which try to legislate the manner in which people may engage in their private sex lives.

A serious effort must be made to distinguish between sin and crime. The Christian community in particular should be slow to call every "crime" a sin and abandon efforts to support its moral convictions about sin with penalties from the criminal code. For example, the unwillingness of many young men in our time to bear arms, or, to be more accurate, to drop bombs on defenseless people, may be a "crime" making them subject to incarceration in a federal penitentiary; but it hardly could be called a sin. To have sexual intercourse with a person whom one pays for this service may be a dehumanizing act for both participants and justly reproved by Christians who see such behavior as a symptom of man's sin. However, a woman engaging in such activity should not be treated by society as a criminal. It is especially unjust that the woman involved and not the man has been prosecuted. Similarly, most arrests for public drunkenness are merely punitive and do not contribute to the desirable rehabilitation of the alcoholic.

Indeed, the confusion of crime and sin has tended to make sin trivial and crime irrelevant and thus detracted from faith as well as justice. Christians have seriously underestimated the power and pervasiveness of sin by believing that their ability to abstain from crime extricated them from the power of sin. The political community, on the other hand, has dabbled in the vain effort to make men moral while neglecting its legitimate responsibility to help and constrain men to act in a safe and responsible manner which would protect the rights of all. It is this latter tendency to use the state as an instrument for the promotion of the moral tenets of one group which has frequently meant that the social and legal reforms available for the reduction of crime have been neglected because of a fundamental confusion of the legitimate tasks of the religious and political communities. One cannot make men just by means of even the best laws and their strictest enforcement, but one can make men act safely and responsibly toward themselves and their neighbors by producing an environment in which such behavior is made relatively easy and rewarding.

It is common knowledge that the most direct and effective way to traffic safety is by means of better roads and safer cars. To teach people to drive carefully on winding and obstructed roads is praiseworthy but far less effective. Yet it is this latter approach which has been commonly used in criminal justice. This approach is particularly self–defeating when dealing with potential and actual criminals since most of them are "born losers" in comparison with those who do not come in conflict with the law. Since education has been a very negative experience for them, an approach which depends mainly upon traditional education to bring about their socialization seems singularly futile.

What is needed is a system which will make it easy to be responsible and law–abiding. Christians will only support such a system if they jettison the popular notion that the medicine that tastes worst is best and that everything which is unpleasant is good for you.

It is essential to mobilize the intelligence and imagination of society to discover ways of making responsible and law–abiding behavior rewarding and thus remove the vast number of secondary crimes which make many of our communities so unsafe. One example must suffice. It is estimated that a heroin addict has to steal $100 worth of goods daily in order to support a moderate habit. If the heroin were administered through clinics with at least 150 outpatients each, the heroin plus administrative costs would total about $4 a day. Based on an estimate of 150,000 opiate addicts in the United States the projected cost to the public in property theft would be $11 billion annually. This would compare with an estimated $450 million to provide a six week in-patient treatment followed by after-care for every opiate addict in the United States. Society, by its obtuse moralistic attitude, encourages both secondary crime and the immensely profitable drug syndicate that promotes drug addiction. Even if very few addicts would be improved by dealing with them through drug rehabilitation clinics and making drugs available to them at cost, the damage to the vicious drug syndicates and the reduction in secondary crimes committed merely to feed the habit would seem to justify the approach.

In order to effect a major change in criminal justice as we know it today, society must accept changes in the design of criminal justice. This can only be accomplished if some of the problems outlined and briefly illustrated above are faced honestly. The Christian community, which has been so influential in creating the ideology upholding the present system—in spite of its reduced influence in a pluralistic America—can play an important part in bringing about necessary change. Christians could contribute much if they would help to clarify the distinction between "crime" and "sin." Religious groups should not try to enforce their special moral precepts through legal means. However, they should insist that the political community furnish rational and prudent explanations acceptable to all men of good will for the legal codes it establishes and enforces. Christians can contribute also by focusing attention on the social and communal causes of crime and foster an attitude toward crime prevention which deals with the actual causes of crime rather than the symptoms.

In all these efforts the basic purpose of criminal justice must be constantly kept in mind—to "protect all members of society, including the offender himself, from seriously harmful and dangerous conduct."[4] For Christians criminal justice systems are one manifestation of God's law in its political function contributing to the preservation of human life and liberty in spite of the destructive and enslaving effects of sin. Such a system must identify and apprehend those who

[4] Roger Ouimet, *Report of the Canadian Committee on Corrections—Toward Unity: Criminal Justice and Corrections* (Ottawa, Ont.: Queen's Printer, 1969), p. 11.

are accused of violating laws duly enacted by the body politic's properly chosen representatives according to a rational and equitable system of justice based on the rights of all men to life, liberty, property, and the pursuit of happiness; prosecute on behalf of the state and guarantee an adequate defense for those charged with criminal activities; and implement sanctions against convicted criminals, such as fines, suspended sentences, compensation to victims, probation, imprisonment, and parole. These functions merit elaboration.

The identification and apprehension of those accused of crime demands methods of inquiry and procedures of apprehension which can easily come in conflict with the basic purpose of criminal justice, namely, to protect all members of society from seriously harmful and dangerous conduct. In the history of mankind, the true criminals of their time have included the agents of absolute monarchies, "democratic" agents during the "reign of terror" of the French Revolution, as well as the secret police and concentration camp guards of Stalinist Russia and Hitlerian Germany.

Police terror is a popular weapon of all "establishments." It starts "harmlessly" with the use of law–enforcement agents for the surveillance of dissenters, the interrogation of newsmen and academies expressing views unpopular with those in power, and it may end with the absolute terror of the modern totalitarian state. It is for this reason of great importance to bring all those activities under the restraint of law and keep them open to public scrutiny. A secret police can hardly be considered a legitimate agent of "law and order." Efforts to identify and apprehend criminals that involve agents of the government in illegal actions (entrapment) may lead to an increase in convictions but generally will hurt the credibility of law enforcement and the dispensation of justice. There may be fewer crimes committed in certain contemporary dictatorships, but the goal does not seem worth the price paid for its achievement. In such settings all citizens are treated as criminals, making the entire country into a top–security prison. The notion that the end justifies the means is theologically unsound, even though advocated by certain so–called Christian ethicists, for it supports the use of evil means for the attainment of vague and uncertain good ends.

Regarding the responsibility of bringing alleged offenders to trial, it is not only important to make every effort to prosecute on behalf of all the people those who have threatened their human rights by dangerous and harmful conduct, but it is equally important that the accused has every opportunity to demonstrate his innocence. Because of the disproportion of power between the government and the accused individual, it is in the interest of all people that the resources of the community be utilized for an adequate defense. To find innocent people guilty is as serious a threat to the administration of justice as the failure to restrain people who are harmful and dangerous to society. Yet a disproportionate amount of public resources is used to prosecute rather than to defend the accused. Although power and resources cannot be equated with justice, a great imbalance of these factors puts at great disadvantage the poor and those of moderate means. They often have no access to the expensive and brilliant private talent which guarantees protection of the rights of the wealthy. But a criminal justice system which metes out full justice to the rich and only occasional justice to the poor tends to undermine all justice. A prevailing opinion holds that the quality of justice depends on the financial resources of the person involved. This public attitude must be changed if the system is to earn the respect of all citizens.

Law without sanctions is empty and meaningless. Criminal justice must apply appropriate sanctions against the guilty promptly if criminal justice is to deter the convicted person from future offenses and motivate him to become a responsible citizen. Justice long delayed is indeed justice denied. But sanctions must be appropriate to the offender and the offense. The tendency to administer more severe punishment for crimes against property than for crimes against persons should be reversed. Christians should take a leading part in this effort because of their relatively high evaluation of persons in comparison to property and their conviction that law was made for the sake of man and not man for the sake of law.

But perhaps one of the important reforms necessary is the compensation of the victims of crime. The entire commonwealth must begin to share the burden which crime places upon its direct victims. Victims of crimes of violence should be restored to health at public expense, and their dependents should be supported by the society whose breakdown was ultimately responsible for their suffering and loss. Victims of crimes against property should be reimbursed up to a reasonable maximum as an expression of the interdependence of all citizens. There is great unfairness in letting a few individuals bear the consequences of the community's failure as a whole. The New Testament exhortation to share one another's burdens should be applied by distributing the real cost of crime more equitably among all citizens. This is especially important in view of the fact that at present a disproportionately great share of crime's cost is borne by those who live in the poorest areas of our cities and are most frequently victims of crimes against persons and property.

But while criminal justice systems are, for Christian theology, a more or less adequate manifestation of the undergirding structure of divine law which maintains human life and culture, Christians are also personally involved in such systems as children of the God who so "loved the world that he gave his only Son, that whoever believes in him should not perish but have eternal life. For God sent the Son into the world, not to condemn the world, but that the world might be saved through him" (John 3:16–17).

The spell of this message should greatly influence Christians in their social relationships and especially in their various contacts with the prevailing system of criminal justice. For Christians love is active in justice, and justice must be seen in the light of God's creative love. This love makes justice possible, and the pervasive and destructive sin of man makes justice necessary.

In our society many participants in the system of criminal justice are in fact Christians. Judges, prosecutors, defense attorneys, members of juries, witnesses, prison administrators, probation and parole officers, teachers in penal institutions, prison chaplains, psychiatrists, psychologists, social workers, and those in academic pursuits related to criminal justice—all may be people who know about the love of God and who are thus under the obligation to see their responsibility in the light of this divine love. As a result they should see their various obligations within the system of criminal justice as opportunities to manifest their faith in a meaningful universe whose ultimate purpose is revealed in the cross and the resurrection of Jesus Christ, and whose God is the God of love. In their participation in the diverse roles assigned to them the reality of the cross should guard them against sentimentality which ignores sin; the reality of the resurrection, against despair which ignores salvation. By constantly overcoming in their several callings the threat of sentimentality and despair they may contribute to the humanization of the formidable and abstract system of criminal justice. They are under a divine call to interpret in society a perspective which sees the conflicts to be resolved, not as conflicts between good and evil, but as the conflicts of fallible and sinful men who are members of one human race (cf. Acts 17:26 ff.).

In this effort, all participants in the criminal justice system, be they administrators of justice or those who are brought unwillingly into the process, insofar as they claim to be Christians must be constantly upheld and guided, supported and reproved by the whole people of God gathered around their Lord. The vision nurtured must be that of a more just world, growing out of their encounter with the Christ who meets, strengthens, and guides them through word and sacrament.

Believing in a Lord who has ruled out vengeance as a proper human motive for action (cf. Rom. 12:14–21), they will use their influence to restrict the objectives of the criminal justice system to the protection of "all members of society from seriously harmful and dangerous conduct."

Christians will be guided here as elsewhere by the role Jesus chose for himself and his disciples: "You know that those who are supposed to rule over the Gentiles lord it over them, and their great men exercise authority over them. But it shall not be so among you; but whoever would be first among you must be slave of all. For the Son of man also came not to be served but to serve, and to give his life as a ransom for many" (Mark 10:42–45). In the context of a modern democratic society such service means involvement in and acceptance of full responsibility for the proper operation and ongoing reform of the criminal justice system. Such efforts at reform may mean entanglement in the ambiguities of politics and give offense to those people inside and outside the churches who would like to restrict Christian concern to the affairs of the world to come. However, the task of the Christian is not the protection of his own moral perfection but rather the service of God in the world and in the person of the neighbor. Such concern is bound to be controversial. In the face of this fact Christians are comforted by the knowledge that being controversial is not "the" sin against the Holy Spirit. They may be strengthened as they remember that Jesus was not the least controversial figure in the Jerusalem of his day.

In the light of the Christian's responsibility to God for his neighbor, certain functions of the criminal justice system deserve special attention. Christians should: work for conditions in which alleged offenders have adequate legal counsel and "due process" is meticulously observed; do everything possible to prevent acts of the governing authorities which are *de facto* punishment when an alleged offender's guilt or innocence has not yet been determined; support every effort to utilize the negative sanctions imposed on convicted offenders as an opportunity to prepare them for a responsible role in society; and cooperate with those individuals and groups who are striving toward an environment in correctional institutions which develops a sense of responsibility and self–acceptance among prisoners.

Because of their responsibility for the weak and defenseless given to them by their Lord (cf. Matt. 25:34–40), Christians must take special interest in the protection and rehabilitation of alleged and convicted offenders. The Christian church as a corporate body and each individual Christian should make every effort to maintain the bonds of common humanity with alleged and convicted offenders. This is especially important since their isolation and alienation from society is a major cause of their difficulties with the law and a main obstacle to their possible rehabilitation.

Since Cain's denial of responsibility for his brother Abel (Gen. 4:9) and Peter's denial of his arrested Lord (Matt. 26:69–75), Christians have been painfully aware of the great pressure to disclaim responsibility for our brothers, particularly those who are in any kind of trouble with the law. Especially if their predicament is caused by their own foolish or culpable acts, we feel justified in ignoring them. Yet our Lord identified himself with us, our own foolishness and culpability notwithstanding. But Christians know that crime is not merely the action of isolated individuals but the result of the common predicament of sinful man in which all share responsibility. Therefore we should lead the way in breaking down the wall between people who are considered criminals by the law and those whom the law considers innocent.

In the presence of the God before whom we live and move and have our being and who has forgiven our sins and made us heirs "and fellow heirs with Christ" (Rom. 8:17), the distinctions between those before and those behind bars lose their absolute significance.

The oneness of humanity at the foot of the cross brings the Christian responsibility for all men and especially the "least of these Christ's brethren" into bold relief. As disciples of him who by his society was accused of receiving sinners and eating with them (Luke 15:2), Christians must show an equal concern for those who are considered harlots, publicans, and sinners in contemporary society. But they shall do this most faithfully if they do it without sentimentality, false rhetoric and illusions concerning the innate goodness of man, using the intelligence God has given them to attack the causes of crime, relieve its victims, and, in so far as humanly possible, restore the offender to useful and joyful participation in the unfinished tasks of the human race.

XII

PARTICULARITY, PLURALISM, AND WORLD COMMUNITY

The concept of particularity is fundamental to the self–understanding of the Christian community. From the very beginning Christians saw themselves as significantly different in their faith from those who were not Christians. This distinctiveness was very marked and very important to them and was implicit in the name "Christian," which they used to describe themselves. The account of St. Paul's sermon at Athens in the Acts of the Apostles shows how in an effort of interpreting the Christian faith to those outside of the community fairly inclusive approaches would be made. In an attempt to establish contact with the audience, the men of Athens were here called *Deisidaimonestezoi*, "very religious." Their worship of an "unknown god" was interpreted positively as establishing a universe of discourse which made communication between Christians and non–Christians possible. Yet the note of particularity entered even into this most inclusive approach. St. Paul, according to the Acts of the Apostles, concluded his sermon with the words:

> The times of ignorance God overlooked, but now he commands all men everywhere to repent, because he has fixed a day on which he will judge the world in righteousness by a man whom he has appointed and of this he has given assurance to all men by raising him from the dead. (Acts 17:30–31)

It is this emphasis on the unique and once-and-for-all character of Jesus as the Christ which establishes Christian particularity. It is explicit in the *hapax* or *ephapax* formulae of Romans 6:10, Hebrews 7:27, 9:12, 9:28, and I Peter 3:18 and the familiar emphasis upon the uniqueness and sufficiency of Jesus as the Christ in John 3:16–17 or the well-known statement in II Corinthians 5:19: "God was in Christ reconciling the world to himself, not counting their trespasses against them and entrusting to us the message of reconciliation."

This Christian assertion of the particularity of the faith is so completely dependent upon their attitude toward Jesus that the Roman Empire in its later persecution of Christians was satisfied to establish the guilt of a person accused as a Christian simply on the basis of his admission that he was a Christian and that he was unwilling to deny Christ. The confession of the name of Christ was crime enough to deserve the death penalty. As Pliny wrote to Emperor Trajan:

> Should the name if free from serious crimes be punished or only the crimes that attach to the name? Pending your advice, the method I have followed with those who were brought before me as Christians is this. I have asked them in person whether they were Christians. If they have confessed I have repeated my inquiry a second and third time, when they persisted I have ordered them to execution.[1]

No effort was made to establish unlawful behavior punishable by death apart from the confession of the name.

It is apparent that it was Christian particularity, the claims made for the person and work of Christ even in the simplest liturgical service, which implicitly denied and subverted the many gods worshipped in the empire. Rejecting their social and political importance the Christians offended and threatened practically everybody. To the degree that these gods were taken seriously for religious, political, or

[1] Epistle XCVI, as quoted in Harold Mattingly, *Christianity in the Roman Empire* (New York: Norton, 1967), p. 37.

traditional reasons Christians were considered carriers of a dangerous plague which, indeed, threatened the survival of ordered society. Christian particularity was seen as both "atheism" and "anarchy." Their attack against certain universally accepted cultural values from the theater to the public baths—which produced the peculiar association of holiness and dirt in early Christian thought revived in our own youth culture—only reinforced the basic suspicion against this "evil and extreme superstition."

When Christianity eventually came to power in the empire its spokesmen insisted that its particular understanding of man's relationship to God was the only correct view. In this attitude they were supported by the political leaders of the time who found a tightly disciplined and ideologically unified religious community most useful for their purposes of preserving a disunited and factious empire. Theological uniformity was even more a political than a religious goal. Only an unambiguous symbol could promise the victory envisioned by Constantine when he saw the words *hoc signo victor eris* in the sky. Indeed, particularity was constantly further refined, became orthodoxy, and led to the persecution of all the non–orthodox, be they schismatics, heretics, adherents of other religions or none at all. As respected and influential a theologian as Augustine of Hippo advocated the forced conversion of the Donatists, saying, "The Church may not only invite but compel men to embrace what is good."[2]

And Thomas Aquinas advocated the killing of sinners after quoting Exodus 22:18, on the principle that the excision of one member for the good of the whole body is praiseworthy. "If a man be dangerous and infectious to the community, on account of some sin, it is praiseworthy and advantageous that he be killed in order to safeguard the

[2] Augustine's "Letter to Donatus," in Forell, *Christian Social Teachings* (New York: Doubleday, 1966), p. 82.

common good."[3] This became the dominant attitude in post–Constantinian Christendom. The Christian faith was not only unique, definable, and true but should if at all possible be enforced everywhere. Even as deviant a prophet as Thomas Münzer proclaimed that "the sword is necessary to wipe out the godless . . . the weeds must be plucked out of the vineyard of God in the time of harvest."[4]

When as a result of the Reformation in the sixteenth-century orthodoxies proliferated in the Western world, this did not at first reduce the absolute claims for their particular visions of the faith. Only when it became apparent that no group had the power to force its particular point of view on all the others was the solution of a multiplicity of particular orthodoxies adopted.

Pluralism, the existence of various and contradictory approaches to life simultaneously, is the long–term result of the break–up of the enforced ideological homogeneity described above. A correlate of secularization, it means that:

> the man in the street is confronted with a wide variety of religious and other reality–defining agencies that compete for his allegiance or at least attention, and none of which is in a position to coerce him into allegiance. In other words, the phenomenon called "pluralism" is a social-structural correlate of the secularization of consciousness.[5]

Precisely because of its long-term commitment to particularity, pluralism presents a special problem to the Christian community. What is to be the Christian attitude toward other reality–defining agencies, including other religions and quasi–religions of the twentieth century? Historically,

---

[3] Thomas Aquinas, *Summa Theologica* as quoted in Forell, *op. cit.*, p. 131.

[4] Thomas Münzer, "Sermon Before the Princes," as quoted in Forell, *op. cit.*, p. 192.

[5] Peter Berger, *The Sacred Canopy* (New York: Doubleday, 1967), p. 126.

Christians have known only two approaches, attempts at isolation and attempts at conversion. One has either ignored the existence of these other ideologies and confined them to an anomic realm outside the concern of Christians, or one has tried to reach them in order to incorporate them by force or persuasion—or a combination of the two—in the *Corpus Christianum*, the small area of meaning within the vast realm meaninglessness. In America, where neither solution was possible because of the variety of reality–defining options within the commonwealth and the unavailability of the power of the state to establish any of them, an effort was made to develop a more inclusive religion, the so–called "Religion of the Republic," which could serve as the reality–defining agency, and combine the essential values of the major religious traditions—Protestant, Catholic, and Jewish. (For a positive evaluation of this developement, see Sidney Mead, *The Lively Experiment.* For a negative view, see Will Herberg, *Protestant, Catholic, and Jew.*)

This "American Religion," however, was just as insistent on its own particularity and eager to establish itself over against other definitions of reality as other religious options. Indeed, until very recently, it supplied the ideological support for the much–discussed efforts to establish an "American Century" or a *Pax Americana.*

But pluralism is here to stay. Thus Christians will have to come to terms with the reality and integrity of other religions and quasi–religions. Can this be done without syncretism or reductionism? It is of the greatest importance to realize that pluralism is not syncretism and does not demand reductionism. The recognition of the rights of others to their religious vision does not imply the renunciation of my own religious hopes or aspirations. Indeed, my own religious insight may give me a valuable clue to the better understanding of the religious commitment of others, just as my own experience of love in the kind of family in which

I have been raised may help me to understand both similar and strikingly different experiences of others.

The recognition and acceptance of religious pluralism does demand the willingness to acknowledge and even cherish religious differences. It excludes the use of force in all its crass and subtle forms to suppress or eliminate them. But it does not remove religion as a subject of discussion among men; indeed, it should encourage it. Dialogue, as openminded and ongoing conversation, is appropriate and imperative lest pluralism deteriorate into isolationism But only if the principle of pluralism is accepted can such dialog be carried on openly and without suspicion.

It is, however, important to realize that pluralism as here described has only become possible as a result of the gradual removal of religion in general and Christianity in particular from the armory of the state. The positive by–product of the much advertised "crisis of credibility in religion for the man on the street is the decreasing pressure on religion to serve as ideology for various political systems. Peter Berger claims that "secularization has resulted in a widespread collapse of the plausibility of religious definitions of reality." This may be the reason that it appears less useful to the political managers of our time for the purpose of cementing the building blocks of their various power structures. This in turn may very well extricate religion from the impending collapse of these systems.

If this analysis has some merit it is important to encourage the further disassociation of Christianity from any political or social establishment, and to emphasize its supernational character. But this also implies a somewhat critical stance in relation to the evolving international power structures.

It is becoming increasingly apparent that the completely sovereign national states which constitute our present world community are non–functional for the survival of the human race. In fact, rather than offering solutions, the sovereign national states are a substantial part of the problem. The various dangers which threaten human extinction have been summarized in the slogan, the ecological crisis of our time. None of the elements of this challenge are subject to unilateral national or even regional attempts at solution. From population explosion to pollution they do not lend themselves to piecemeal answers; they demand a responsible world community politically organized so as to act on behalf of the interests of all men and thus ultimately on behalf of all forms of life. It has become obvious that reverence for all life is today a postulate of practical human reason.

Under such circumstances it seems urgent that all men of good will should use the resources of their "reality-defining agencies," their religions and quasi-religions in order to support the development of a viable world community able to cope with these challenges.

But past experience with serving as ideological support for a *Pax Romana* or more recently *Pax Americana* should make Christians, at least, very cautious about the manner of their involvement in agencies establishing and enforcing universal peace and welfare. While Christians should certainly try to generate support for national and international policies which contribute to the building of a world community, they should not do so unilaterally, nor identify such a policy with the Christian gospel. The Christian churches' experience of serving as the exclusive and publicly supported reality-defining agency in post–Constantinian Europe should make all Christians suspicious about any institutional involvement in "One-World Construction" and "One-World Maintenance."

While Christians should indeed support justice and peace and all efforts to establish a viable and stable world order, they should not even try to give specifically Christian sanction to any or all of these efforts. It is the task of the Christian community to live and proclaim its faith in Jesus, the Christ, as the disclosure of the meaning, purpose, and ultimate destiny of each human life in the plan of God—to state their vision that God was in Christ reconciling the world unto himself. This may have all kinds of important communal and personal consequences for their participation in efforts to create world community and to support world order. But it should be done without impugning or co-opting the vision of others, which may be equally supportive of these aims. In other words, the particular Christian vision should be upheld in open acceptance of pluralism. In a world which is rapidly becoming a neighborhood in which all men will have to live as brothers, the gospel should be proclaimed without demanding or offering to have it serve as the social or political ideology for anybody, even a world community.

If Christians have learned anything from the past they should have learned modesty. If it is asserted that contemporary Christian claims presenting specifically Christian solutions to all man's earthly problems are different from those of the past because they are so well–intended, one ought to remember that the claims of the past were well–intended as well.

There is nothing intrinsically wrong with particularity if it is accepted in the context of pluralism and thus does not infringe on the particularity of others. In fact, such particularity may indeed support and enrich the world community of tomorrow.